THE
DISRUPTORS

TECHNOLOGY–DRIVEN
ARCHITECT–ENTREPRENEURS

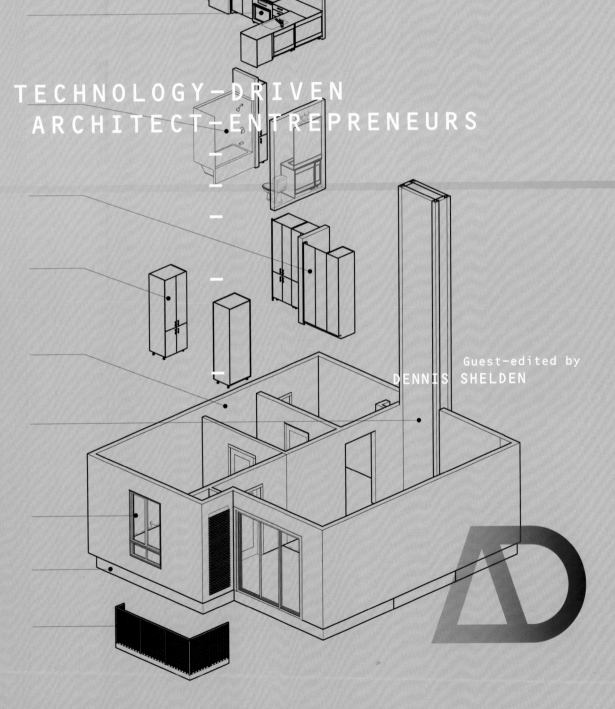

Guest–edited by
DENNIS SHELDEN

AD

02 | Vol 90 | 2020

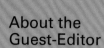

About the Guest-Editor

Dennis Shelden

05

Introduction
Entrepreneurial Practice

New Possibilities for a Reconfiguring Profession

Dennis Shelden

06

Empowering Design

Gehry Partners, Gehry Technologies, and Architect-Led Industry Change

Frank Gehry, Meaghan Lloyd and Dennis Shelden

14

The Evolution of a Specialised Practice

Consulting and Contracting in the Integrated Envelope Delivery Industry

Marc Simmons

24

New Models of Building

The Business of Technology

David Fano and Daniel Davis

32

Disrupting from the Inside

UK Archipreneurs

Helen Castle

40

Design, Data and Liveability

The Role of Technology Within the Future of an Expanded Profession

Ben van Berkel

58

Is Bigger Better?

The Rise of Specialisation in Professional Practice

James P Cramer and Scott Simpson

50

Mind the Gap

Architecture and the Absurdity of Self-Imposed Limitation

Brad Samuels

66

CetraRuddy, Lincoln Square Synagogue, New York City, 2013

Salmela Architect, Family Retreat, Duluth, Minnesota, 2018

ISSN 0003-8504
ISBN 978 1119 555094

Guest-edited by **Dennis Sheldon**

Collaborative Networks of Robotic Construction

Philip F Yuan and Chao Yan

74

The Distractions of Disruptions

Technical Supply in an Era of Social Demand

Phil Bernstein

82

Better Development

Alternative Value Creation

Jared Della Valle

88

Architecture at Scale

Reimagining One-Off Projects as Building Platforms

Craig Curtis

96

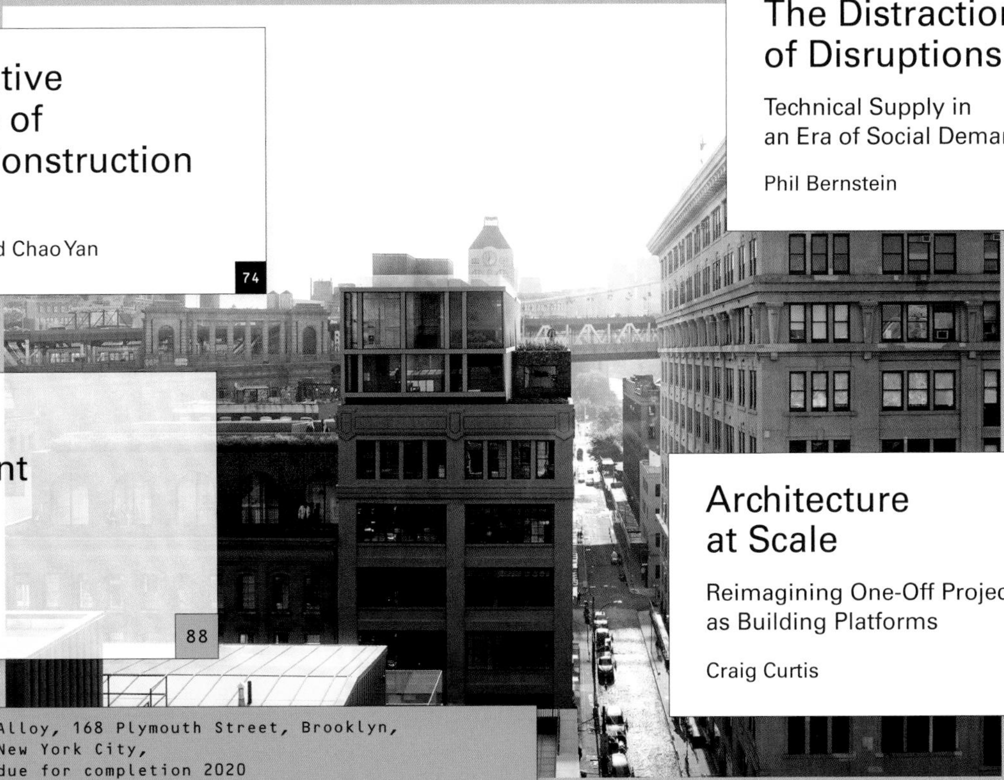

Automation and Machine Learning in Architecture

A New Agenda for Performance-Driven Design

Sandeep Ahuja and Patrick Chopson

104

Anti-Entrepreneurs

Using Computation to Unscale Production

Jesse Louis-Rosenberg and Jessica Rosenkrantz

112

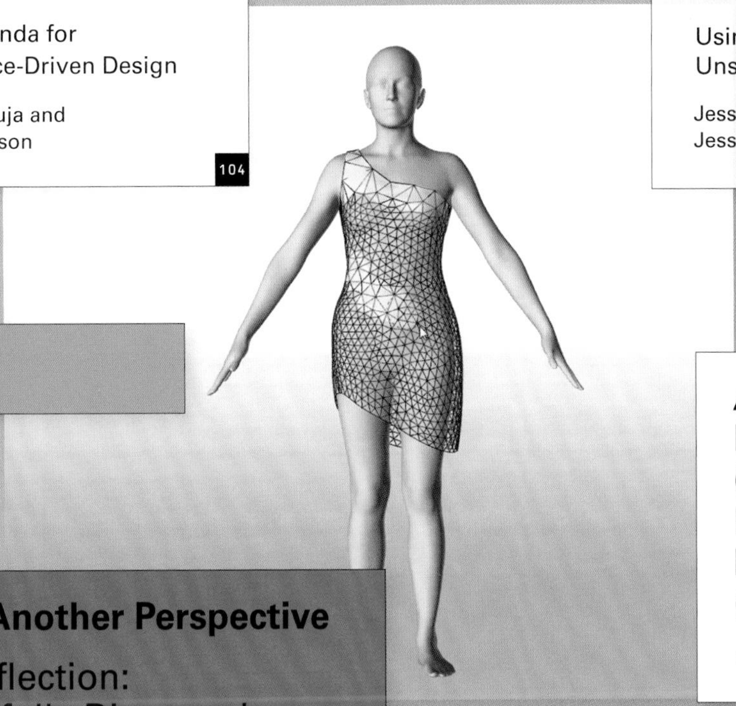

Architects = Innovators (sometimes) Innovators ≠ Entrepreneurs (most of the time)

Greg Lynn

120

From Another Perspective

On Reflection: Beautifully Disrupted Architectural Art

Neil Spiller

128

Contributors

134

Alloy, 168 Plymouth Street, Brooklyn, New York City, due for completion 2020

Nervous System, Kinematics Cloth app, 2014

Editorial Offices
John Wiley & Sons
9600 Garsington Road
Oxford
OX4 2DQ

T +44 (0)1865 776868

Editor
Neil Spiller

Commissioning Editor
Helen Castle

Managing Editor
Caroline Ellerby
Caroline Ellerby Publishing

Freelance Contributing Editor
Abigail Grater

Publisher
Paul Sayer

Art Direction + Design
CHK Design:
Christian Küsters
Barbara Nassisi

Production Editor
Elizabeth Gongde

Prepress
Artmedia, London

Printed in Italy by Printer
Trento Srl

Front cover: UNStudio
and SCAPE, Prototype
RESET Stress Reduction
Pods, Salone del
Mobile, Milan, Italy, 2017.
© Oddproduzioni

Inside front cover: Katerra
advanced manufacturing
facility, Phoenix, Arizona,
2019. © Katerra

Page 1: Jennifer Fontenot,
Jeremy Jacinth and
Brittany Olivari, A+Design,
Exploring New Value
Propositions for Design
Practice, Yale School of
Architecture, New Haven,
Connecticut, 2017.
© Jennifer Fontenot,
Jeremy Jacinth and
Brittany Olivari

02/2020

⅄D ARCHITECTURAL DESIGN

March/April 2020

Profile No. 264

Disclaimer
The Publisher and Editors cannot be held responsible
for errors or any consequences arising from the use
of information contained in this journal; the views and
opinions expressed do not necessarily reflect those of
the Publisher and Editors, neither does the publication
of advertisements constitute any endorsement by
the Publisher and Editors of the products advertised.

Journal Customer Services
For ordering information,
claims and any enquiry
concerning your journal
subscription please go to
www.wileycustomerhelp
.com/ask or contact your
nearest office.

Americas
E: cs-journals@wiley.com
T: +1 781 388 8598 or
+1 800 835 6770 (toll free
in the USA & Canada)

**Europe, Middle East
and Africa**
E: cs-journals@wiley.com
T: +44 (0)1865 778315

Asia Pacific
E: cs-journals@wiley.com
T: +65 6511 8000

Japan (for Japanese-
speaking support)
E: cs-japan@wiley.com
T: +65 6511 8010 or 005 316
50 480 (toll-free)

Visit our Online Customer
Help available in 7 languages
at www.wileycustomerhelp
.com/ask

Print ISSN: 0003-8504
Online ISSN: 1554-2769

Prices are for six issues
and include postage and
handling charges. Individual-
rate subscriptions must be
paid by personal cheque or
credit card. Individual-rate
subscriptions may not be
resold or used as library
copies.

All prices are subject to
change without notice.

Identification Statement
Periodicals Postage paid
at Rahway, NJ 07065.
Air freight and mailing in
the USA by Mercury Media
Processing, 1850 Elizabeth
Avenue, Suite C, Rahway,
NJ 07065, USA.

USA Postmaster
Please send address changes
to *Architectural Design*,
John Wiley & Sons Inc.,
c/o The Sheridan Press,
PO Box 465, Hanover,
PA 17331, USA

Subscribe to ⅄D
⅄D is published bimonthly
and is available to purchase
on both a subscription basis
and as individual volumes
at the following prices.

Prices
Individual copies:
£29.99 / US$45.00
Individual issues on
⅄D App for iPad:
£9.99 / US$13.99
Mailing fees for print
may apply

Annual Subscription Rates
Student: £90 / US$137
print only
Personal: £136 / US$215
print and iPad access
Institutional: £310 / US$580
print or online
Institutional: £388 / US$725
combined print and online
6-issue subscription on
⅄D App for iPad: £44.99 /
US$64.99

Dennis Shelden is a building professional, academic, author and entrepreneur whose experience spans architecture, engineering and computer-science applications in professional practice and the built environment. He lectures and publishes widely on topics of computational applications in architecture, and building industry transformation. He holds degrees from the Massachusetts Institute of Technology (MIT): a Bachelor of Science in Art and Design with a concentration in Architectural Design; Master of Science in Civil and Environmental Engineering; and a Doctor of Philosophy in Architecture: Computation and Design, under the guidance of William J Mitchell.

He joined Gehry Partners in 1997 while still in MIT's PhD programme, first as Director of Research and Development, then as Director of Computing, and was responsible for the management and strategic direction of the firm's computing programme, including software and process development, research, IT infrastructure and partnerships. His PhD thesis 'Digital Surface Representation and the Constructability of Gehry's Architecture' (2002) remains a widely referenced treatise on the motivations and technical underpinnings of the firm's revolutionary digital approach to the design and delivery of complex buildings. After completing his PhD, he co-founded the spinoff company Gehry Technologies, served as Chief Technology Officer, led the development of several software products, and was Project Executive on numerous groundbreaking building projects until the firm's acquisition by Trimble in 2014. Prior to joining Gehry Partners he held diverse positions including performing structural and environmental engineering at Arup, real-time optimisation of building energy systems at Consultants' Computation Bureau, and development of the first laser-based point cloud scanner at Cyra Systems, since acquired by Leica.

He is an Associate Professor of Architecture and Director of Rensselaer Polytechnic Institute's Center for Architecture, Science and Ecology (CASE) in New York City. His work focuses on professional applications of generative and building information modelling to the design, construction and operation of integrated physical/digital building systems, including built environment, Internet of Things (IoT) and Digital Twin applications. Before leading CASE he was Associate Professor of Architecture, Director of the Digital Building Laboratory and Director of the School of Architecture's Doctoral programme at Georgia Tech, Associate Professor of Practice in MIT's Design and Computation Program and held teaching positions at the University of California, Los Angeles (UCLA) and the Southern California Institute of Architecture (SCI-Arc). He co-directs the technical programme for buildingSMART International, the building industries' open information standards body, where he leads efforts to develop technology platforms for open data web- and cloud-based building design, construction and operations systems.

His publications have appeared in journals including *D*, *TAD: Technology and Architectural Design*, and the *Journal of Construction Automation*, and he has been interviewed by publications including the *Economist, New York Times, Design Intelligence* and *Engineering News Record*. He is editor of the forthcoming book series *Practical Revolutions: Professional Building Applications of Disruptive Technologies*, published by John Wiley & Sons. *D*

ENTREPRENEURIAL PRACTICE

NEW POSSIBILITIES FOR A RECONFIGURING PROFESSION

INTRODUCTION

DENNIS SHELDEN

At the end of the 20th century, the building industry was broken.

In 1998 the landmark Egan Report was commissioned by the UK government.[1] The study exemplified a message prevalent at the time that still echoes today. The building design and construction industry was fundamentally broken: fragmented into many small firms – regionalism institutionalised by the idiosyncrasies of local building codes and agencies, subject to low bid requirements that encourage rather than prevent cost overruns and litigation, and characterised by extremely low investment in innovation. A ubiquitously cited 1999 study compared building construction's downward trend in efficiency with the exponential technology-driven growth in efficacy and value of other economic sectors.[2] The features of this dysfunction – fragmentation, risk aversion, low investment and low compensation – were well known and to a great extent persist today. But no clear remedies could be identified, and the same impediments to change created something of a safe harbour for traditional models of practice to resist the economic imperative of advancement.

Early Pioneers

In the early 2000s, new companies began to pursue opportunities within and across the gaps in the industry. Gehry Technologies (see pp 14–23) was formed in 2002 as a spin-off from Frank Gehry's architectural practice; SHoP Construction similarly emerged from SHoP Architects. Two of Front's (pp 24–31) founders met while working at Foster + Partners. Shortly after, CASE (pp 32–9) was formed by Federico Negro, David Fano and Steve Sanderson, who had met and begun working at SHoP. These firms were started by architects to serve the building design and construction industries through services not easily characterised in terms of traditional roles. Technology was the common theme, and they were formed at a time when 3D computer-aided design (CAD) and building information modelling (BIM) were evolving into first-tier drivers of advanced building. Only some were first and foremost technology providers. All grew and thrived during the acceleration of possibility and demand for geometrically complex buildings forms enabled by a set of powerful new tools.

These practices were not singularly unique – in innovation, technology focus or as architect entrepreneurs. Much earlier in the 1990s, Skidmore, Owings & Merrill (SOM) pioneered the development of software products by an architectural practice. Innovative practices such as Zaha Hadid Architects (ZHA), Foster + Partners and Kohn Pedersen Fox (KPF) were achieving renown for work accelerated by home-grown technical advances that

Sidewalk Labs,
Quayside,
Sidewalk Toronto,
Toronto,
2017–

Sidewalk Labs is a heavily funded Google-affiliated startup pursuing smart city developments. Sidewalk Toronto is its first urban development proposal located in Toronto's Eastern Waterfront. The development tackles the challenges of urban growth and aims to make the city a global hub for urban innovation.

allowed both signature formal expression and a capacity for global delivery. And large, integrated conglomerates were beginning to form – with AECOM among the most visible.

But common among the new startups and spin-offs was a theme of technology-driven, architect-led entrepreneurship: the identification of a new, unfilled opportunity in the industry, disclosed by advanced knowledge of practice, and served by commercial ventures distinct from traditional modes of practice. These firms were founded on the premise that non-traditional entities were needed to fill the gaps between traditional designers and builders. Adopting these offerings required exceptional circumstances: high-profile, complex and risky projects, often led by singular visionary project owners who knew that 'safer' methods were riskier than trying a different approach, were willing to be the magnets for risk associated with change, and had the ambition to take control and lead.

Of these firms, today only Front remains in business as a standalone company. Gehry Technologies and CASE were acquired, respectively, by Trimble and WeWork, larger technology-driven companies with very different businesses. SHoP Construction was closed in 2015, but its founders have gone on to start other ventures. Even Front has returned to its more traditional roots as a specialist enclosure consultancy. As the markets, technologies and capacities of the profession caught up with the unique capacities of these firms, they evolved, closed or chose to align themselves with larger, better-funded organisations.

Paul Teicholz,
Labour productivity in construction,
1999

Teicholz's frequently cited study of US construction industry productivity versus that of other sectors provides a stark visualisation of the lingering inefficiencies in the building industry over the course of the information technology revolution. The study, entitled 'Reverse Productivity Declines', was first published, in *Engineering News-Record*, in December 1999.

Construction and Non-Farm Labor Productivity Index (1964-2003)
Constant $ of contracts / workhours of hourly workers
Sources: US Dept. of Commerce, Bureau of Labor Statistics

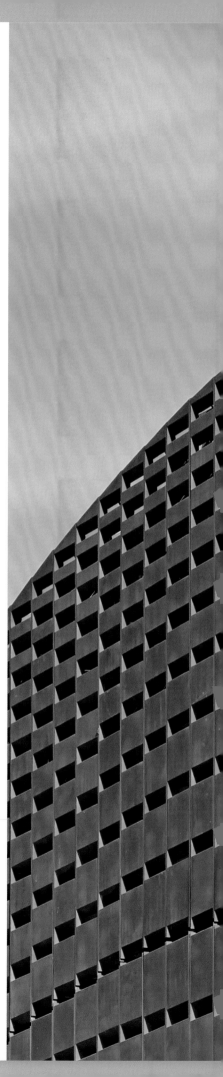

—Construction Productivity Index   (1964 = 100 %)
—Cumulative Non-Farm Productivity Index

SHoP,
Barclays Center,
Brooklyn, New York,
2012

SHoP Architects created a separate company, SHoP Construction, to
assist in the delivery of buildings during fabrication and construction
on projects including the Barclays Center. The project features a
facade comprising 12,000 unique metal panels. A model-based
digital-delivery process was developed to streamline the design and
delivery of the panels with direct output of digital instructions for
their fabrication and assembly.

Technology and Disruption

In the ensuing years, technology-driven disruption and the associated reconfiguration of industries and cultures has emerged as a key characteristic of modern society. The narrative of startups, entrepreneurship, market disruption and capital-driven growth has become ubiquitous in the tech industry and impacted industries from advertising and music to transportation. The 'hero' innovators, from Steve Jobs and Bill Gates to Larry Page, Mark Zuckerberg and Elon Musk, have become part of the 21st-century cultural narrative, eclipsing the robber barons, industrialists and entertainment stars of the 20th century. Counter-culturalists such as Tim Berners-Lee and Edward Snowden are resisting the siren song of wealth and power as a driving motivation for tech-driven societal change. The escalating duality of technology-driven advancement and destruction has become endemic to modern life and our visions of possible futures.

In 2016–17, the management consulting firms Boston Consulting Group,[3] McKinsey[4] and KPMG all produced widely distributed reports heralding building design and construction as the next industry for tech-driven disruption. Significant and growing investment capital has come into the market, with Softbank – the world's largest investment fund – leading the way. A number of smaller venture funds are emerging to invest specifically in building industry initiatives: some 'angels' who achieved success in last-generation building industry software; others, such as Thornton Tomasetti's TTWiiN incubator, springing out of traditional building construction and product companies. In the last three years there has been an exponential acceleration of such startups tackling built environment opportunities.

It is clear that the dynamics of entrepreneurialism and disruption are taking root in the building industries, driven by a number of forces. The pent-up demand for increased value from the dollars spent and the resources deployed in buildings is one of them. The huge scale of the built environment and the latent inefficiency in this economic sector is attracting the interest of 'disruptors' who have achieved transformational success tackling large problems in other sectors. It is also becoming apparent that the built environment itself is a platform for technology and data innovation. Ventures such as Sidewalk Labs are among the most visible of those who see the built environment as the platform by which new technologies will be deployed into the world. And, the visible contributions of the built environment to climate change and a growing demand by governments – spearheaded by Europe and Asia – to address these impacts are creating identifiable new opportunities for optimisation of building delivery and operations.

Of all the existing parties in traditional practice, architects are both the most likely potential victims of disruption as well as the most promising potential leaders of transformational change. The act of an individual or small group foraying out to start their own practice is a singularly entrepreneurial act, and has been central to the narrative, growth and evolution of the profession. Architects are trained in the thought process of creativity emerging from a disparate set of existing conditions – cultural, economic, physical, information and policy – assembled, mixed and formed into wholly new solutions through a set of techniques that combine ideation, analysis, testing, discarding and reinventing. Architects create vast amounts of new intellectual property over the course of design – new concepts, inventions and methods – and are perhaps uniquely positioned to holistically take on problems and opportunities identified in the broader culture of resources and finances, people and technologies, natural and artificial systems.

Yet architecture as a profession is also culturally adverse – even wilfully naive – to the contemporary forces and possibilities of disruption. The legislative and contractual tendencies of the profession have evolved the role of the architect to one of overall input but increasingly limited agency – with protection from risk diminishing access to the flow of finance and associated control of project sums. The intentionally adversarial relationship between architects, project managers and contractors – coupled with the limited risk profile, authority and economic compensation in design-bid-build – places architects at an economic and control disadvantage in driving change. Despite the innovation and intellectual property it generates, the profession has few traditional mechanisms for defending and leveraging this IP across projects, and ideas are quickly copied by others. In addition, the boom-and-bust cycle of projects make scaling and investing in people and ideas difficult over the long term.

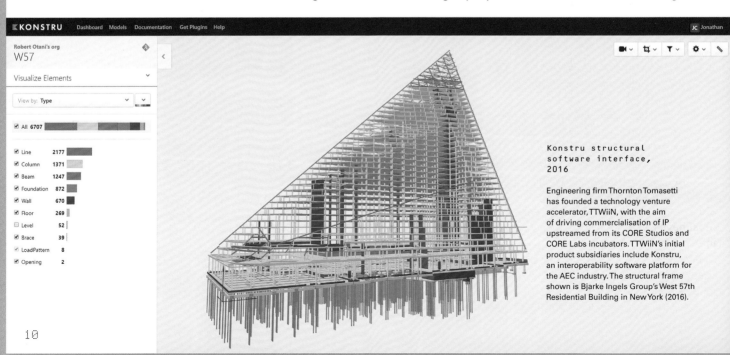

Konstru structural software interface, 2016

Engineering firm Thornton Tomasetti has founded a technology venture accelerator, TTWiiN, with the aim of driving commercialisation of IP upstreamed from its CORE Studios and CORE Labs incubators. TTWiiN's initial product subsidiaries include Konstru, an interoperability software platform for the AEC industry. The structural frame shown is Bjarke Ingels Group's West 57th Residential Building in New York (2016).

Tech-Enabled Architect-Entrepreneurs
It is this accelerating climate of entrepreneurial disruption
and technology-driven response that this issue of Δ takes
on, with the specific hypothesis of the architect as a driver of
entrepreneurial change. The assembled contributors represent
a broad swath of innovators who are exploring alternatives
for practice and for the profession. Some – including Frank
Gehry, David Fano and Daniel Davis from the technology
service company CASE, and Marc Simmons from the
envelope consultancy Front – come from the original group of
innovative practices formed at the beginning of architecture's
digital expansion. Others, including Brad Samuels's SITU,
Philip Yuan's Archi-Union, and the firms discussed by Helen
Castle, Jim Cramer and Scott Simpson, represent a new
generation of architectural practices. Jesse Louis-Rosenberg
and Jessica Rosenkrantz (Nervous System), Sandeep Ahuja
and Patrick Chopson (Pattern r+d) and Greg Lynn are architects
or engineers that have taken their practices into product-
focused directions. Jared Della Valle at Alloy and Craig Curtis
at Katerra are architects by background who have created or
are leading integrated design-build-owner organisations.
Most have been educators, authors and critics exploring
innovative ideas for practice in the context of studios and in
their writing, exemplified by Phil Bernstein's entrepreneurial
academic initiatives, and Philip F Yuan and Chao Yan's
innovation networks.

Piaggio Fast Forward,
gita robot,
2019

Architect Greg Lynn has applied design thinking and technology
innovation in diverse projects, from building design to furniture.
Current ventures include Piaggio Fast Forward – a spin-off from the
Italian motor-vehicle manufacturer Piaggio, which has produced a
robotic hands-free carrier that can recognise and follow its owner.

It is this accelerating
climate of
entrepreneurial
disruption and
technology-driven
response that
this issue of
Δ takes on

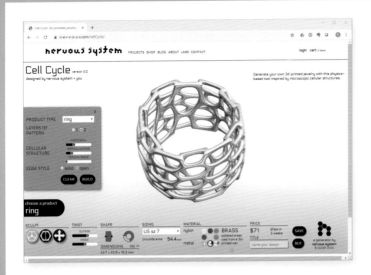

Nervous System,
Cell Cycle,
2009-

left: Founded in 2007 by Jessica Rosenkrantz and Jesse Louis-Rosenberg, Nervous System has pioneered the application of new technologies in design, including generative systems, 3D printing, and webGL. The studio releases online design applications that enable customers to co-create products in an effort to make design more accessible. These tools allow for endless design variation and customisation. The Cell Cycle online design tool allows users to design custom jewellery on the Web. The design is 3D printed, cast in metal and shipped to the user. Cell Cycle represents a new approach to manufacturing that tightly integrates design, simulation and digital fabrication to create complex, customised products.

Gehry Technologies,
Digital Project,
2007

Gehry Partners' offshoot tech company Gehry Technologies supports the firm's extended project teams and brings 3D digital delivery advances to the building industry. Digital Project – a parametric BIM software application – was first released in 2004 through a partnership with aerospace software company Dassault Systèmes.

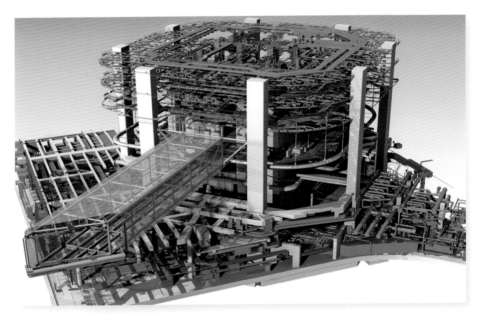

UNStudio / UNSense,
Brainport Smart District,
Helmond,
The Netherlands,
2018

Architectural practice UNStudio has founded a spin-off company, UNSense, the goal of which is to bring to market the technology innovations emerging out of the practice's design projects. The companies partner on many projects, but have different areas of focus, and are structured separately to support the necessary dynamics of the architecture and tech business models. Both are heavily involved in the physical and system designs for smart cities including the Brainport Smart District of 1,500 houses that will be able to generate almost all of its own services.

The breadth of these contributors' experiences elides easy characterisation or takeaway lessons. However, a few themes emerge from their writings. First, technology and the market forces of entrepreneurialism, invention and disruption can be harnessed to empower the architectural agenda. For Gehry, the creation of tools to support a creative process enables new ways of building, differentiation and brand identity, but more importantly a means for architects to reclaim authority and control. For Della Valle and Curtis, controlling the capital of project ownership provides the agency to redeploy the value of construction towards cultural and design interests.

The prevalent narrative of the tech world – of the relentless pursuit of scale as a consequence of disruptive entrepreneurship – is not a necessary outcome. Nervous System, Front and Alloy are taking advantage of the power of alternative modes of practice, and increasing their capacity and reach, without pursuing exponential growth.

Entrepreneurial firms need to be nimble. A number of the contributors to this issue describe a rolling sequence of areas of focus and business models in companies like SITU, Front, Gehry Technologies and UNSense, the technology incubator spin-off of architectural practice UNStudio. The challenge of developing and leading organisations that can continuously evolve while maintaining a persistent and defensible core ethos and distinguished capabilities is one of the most challenging aspects of practice innovation.

Architecture and design are broadly applicable beyond the narrow dimensional bounds of the building scale and the narrow role of designers and generators of prescriptive information fulfilled by others. Greg Lynn has developed products in parallel with his architectural practice and is now CEO of a transport company. Louis-Rosenberg and Rosenkrantz's work at Nervous System ranges from fashion to medical instruments. UNSense increasingly creates both human-scale devices as well as new cities.

Finally, the macro cultural forces of technological, climate and social change are increasing – not decreasing – demand for the socially oriented values of the profession. This is central to the experiences described by Ben van Berkel of UNStudio in launching UNSense. In his essay, Simmons describes an evolution through many modes of practice to arrive at a set of capabilities that can be deployed to solve new and pressing local and global humanitarian challenges.

Disruption and the Reassertion of Architecture

If the hypotheses and examples of the contributors to this 𝔇 are a correct predictor of architecture's future, the next decades will be a period of radically accelerated disruption and change for the profession. The traditional, fragmented models of practice will be dramatically rewritten by integrated or alternative ones. A spectrum of new directions for careers, firm orientations and business models will be available and in fact required of both firm leaders and the next generation of students entering into the profession. A host of new materials, methods, building types and inventions will become integral to the delivery of buildings. The macro humanistic and ecological forces of climate change, humanitarian crises and economic stratification will become urgent and central questions. These new demands and capacities will create an imperative for adaption and evolution by firms and the profession at large. But these opportunities and the means for seizing them – including access to technology, capital and global markets – will be increasingly within the potential reach of architects. If these predictions are true, it becomes vital that architecture confronts rather than retracts from these opportunities as both a means for survival and to continue to assert the values of our profession in the next era of society. The contributors to this issue show this can be done. 𝔇

It becomes vital that architecture confronts rather than retracts from these opportunities as both a means for survival and to continue to assert the values of our profession in the next era of society

Notes
1. John Egan, *Rethinking Construction: Report of the Construction Task Force*, HMSO (London), November 1998. See: http://constructingexcellence.org.uk/wp-content/uploads/2014/10/rethinking_construction_report.pdf.
2. Paul Teicholz, 'Reverse Productivity Declines', *Engineering News-Record*, 13 December 1999, p 59.
3. *Shaping the Future of Construction: A Breakthrough in Mindset and Technology*, World Economic Forum and Boston Consulting Group, May 2016: www3.weforum.org/docs/WEF_Shaping_the_Future_of_Construction_full_report__.pdf.
4. Filipe Barbosa *et al*, *Reinventing Construction Through a Productivity Revolution*, McKinsey Global Institute, February 2017: www.mckinsey.com/industries/capital-projects-and-infrastructure/our-insights/reinventing-construction-through-a-productivity-revolution.

Text © 2020 John Wiley & Sons Ltd. Images: pp 6-7 courtesy Sidewalk Labs; p 8(l) © Paul Teicholz; pp 8(r)-9 © Bruce Damonte. All rights reserved; p 10 © Thornton Tomasetti; p 11 Piaggio Fast Forward © 2019; p 12(t) © Nervous System; p 12(c) image courtesy of Gehry Technologies; p 12(b) © UNStudio

Frank Gehry, Meaghan Lloyd and Dennis Shelden

EMPOW DESIGN

GEHRY PARTNERS, GEHRY TECHNOLOGIES, AND ARCHITECT-LED INDUSTRY CHANGE

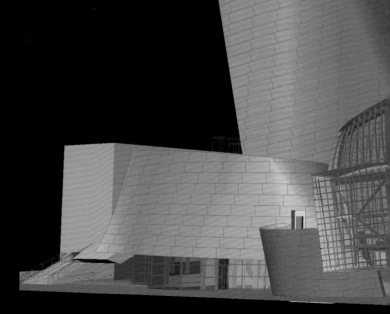

Gehry Partners,
Walt Disney Concert Hall,
Los Angeles,
California,
2002

In the 1990s, Gehry Partners pioneered the
development of its Digital Master Model software
and project delivery approach, enabling the
realisation of its building projects and resulting
in the creation of its software development and
consulting spinoff Gehry Technologies.

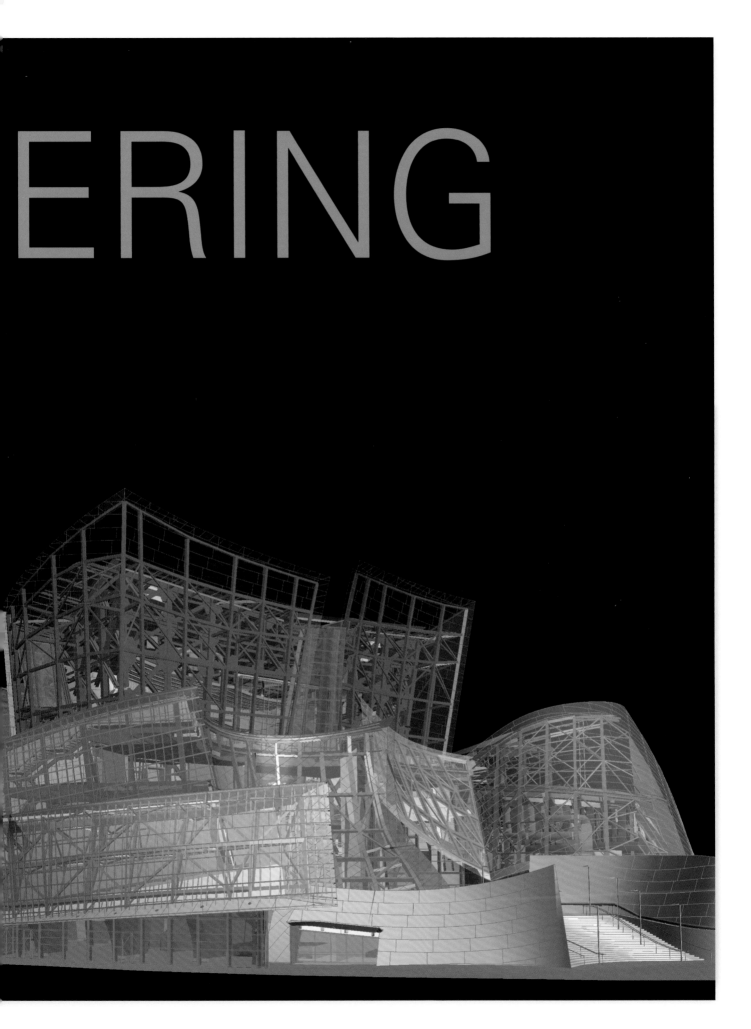

ERING

Since the early 1990s, Gehry Partners has pioneered the development of digital design. The firm's approach to digitally enhanced architecture necessitated the creation of Gehry Technologies. Here, **Frank Gehry**, with former Gehry Technologies chief executive officer **Meaghan Lloyd** and chief technology officer **Dennis Shelden**, describe the motivations, history and implications of these efforts for practice and for the profession.

For Gehry Partners (GP), digital technology has always been about making better architecture. Frank has always believed that an architect's job does not end with the design. In his words:

The client hires us and expects that we are going to be parental through the whole process to make sure that they get the building they want for the price they want to pay. I believe that far too many architects have ceded their responsibility to less interested parties, which results in compromises in design or budget over-runs. I have spent 40 years building my architecture practice to be the Master Builder for my clients and I opened my tech company up to other architects to help them realise the same benefits for their clients.

The process of building buildings has not always served clients or architecture. A design has to go through thousands of hands before it is built. The design intent has to flow through engineers, consultants, project managers and contractors, who are all adding their own information to the documents. Along that path, there are many places where the information can be misinterpreted, misaligned and generally messed up. If the documentation of the design is not well coordinated, it can result in a lot of wasted time and money.

Great buildings require this precision in order to realise the vision in a cost-effective way. Great buildings do not need to cost a lot, but they do involve risk, and they require everyone on the project to hold hands and jump off the cliff together to create something new.

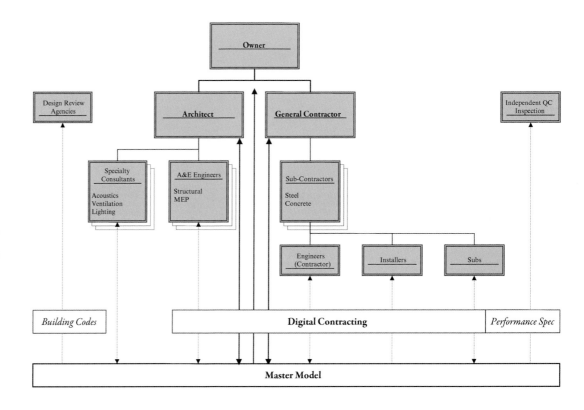

Gehry Partners, Master Model delivery approach, 2002

In the late 1990s and early 2000s, Gehry Partners developed an approach to the design and delivery of its projects, using a central 3D model tying together the work of its extended project team.

Technology has allowed Gehry Partners to take these risks, to work with others on projects that aspire to do great things, and to reduce the risk of doing something unprecedented. The systems and materials the firm uses are often standard building systems, but ones that have seldom been used in exactly the same way before, pushed to their natural limits. Digital tools have allowed the firm to take normal ways of building, apply them in ways never before done, demonstrate to the rest of the team that these are in fact normal systems, and translate the designs back into the documentation languages familiar to the trades.

In the late 1990s, Gehry Partners started working with the aerospace software company Dassault Systèmes using their CATIA® software. CATIA had many more capabilities than the few other architect-focused products that were in existence at the time. CATIA was focused on connecting from design to fabrication in a distributed supply chain, allowing the designed shapes to be expanded into very specific details – all the way down to the bolt and fillet. It had abilities to form and unfold surface materials onto shapes and could be curved and cut into subsystems and drawings without degrading the geometry.

Building the Master Model
The firm arrived at an approach to the delivery of its buildings called the Master Model process, where a primary physical model was maintained as the main record of the design in the physical studio and a corresponding digital model was made by digitising the physical model using a 3D arm that captured points and curves of the shape. This became the 3D Master Model, which captured not only the architecture but also the rest of the primary systems such as the structure, the mechanical, electrical and plumbing (MEP) systems, vertical transportation, etc. Instructions for how the models were to be relied on were included in the project documents.

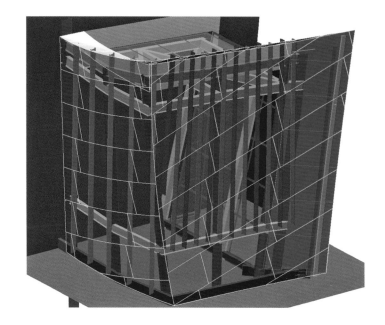

Gehry Partners,
Walt Disney Concert Hall,
Los Angeles, California,
2002

Digital and physical performance mock-ups for the Disney Concert Hall. The process of working through the delivery and performance testing of a portion of the project allows the design qualities, system performance and delivery process to be worked through in advance of contracting and construction.

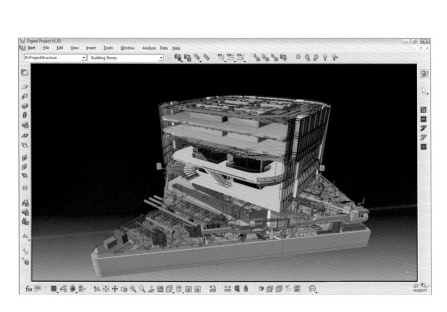

Wang & Ouyang,
One Island East project,
Hong Kong,
2008

The Digital Project software used for this image was developed by Gehry Technologies using the CATIA V5 engine. Digital Project brought scalable parametric modelling with design-to-fabrication innovations from aerospace and manufacturing to the building industries.

The Guggenheim Bilbao (1997) was a turning point for the firm and its Master Model approach, where the unique ways of working became visible to many in the design and construction world. This project, which was built in northern Spain, came in on time and under budget using the digital delivery system. Frank knew that this new process was going to work when bids from the three prospective steel contractors – none of whom had digital experience – came in within a 1 per cent spread of each other and 18 per cent under the budget. This type of precision was rare in rectilinear buildings, let alone buildings such as the Guggenheim.

The Walt Disney Concert Hall in Los Angeles (2003) cemented the role of the Master Model approach to digital project delivery as an enabler of creativity and control. Repeatedly, the digital tools have allowed the firm to defend the feasibility of the design and proposed systems and to bring these seemingly complex buildings in on a rational schedule and with a rational budget. In order to do this, large physical mock-ups are built from the 3D models in order to work through the details process with fabricators. Seeing the results go from 3D to fully built in the physical world with such accuracy and consistency was very convincing to fabricators, owners and builders. This success gave them the confidence to work with Gehry Partners on the firm's projects with the firm's digital delivery process. Indeed, many of the firm's clients and consultants were early adopters of the digital delivery process themselves.

Gehry Partners brought all of this to bear on the construction of 8 Spruce Street in New York (2011). Detailed work with the curtain wall consultant in the design and construction document phase translated into a very smooth construction process. The highly curved facade with 10,500 unique panels was bid out at the same price as a flat glass curtain wall in New York City and it was built without any change orders. The concrete work had only eight change orders. The general rule of thumb is that change orders account for about 15 per cent of any project cost, so the close coordination paid off. It was a financial coup for the client as well. In a downward-trending market, the project leased quickly and has done well for them over the years. Good design and good process is good business.

Gehry Partners' relationship with Dassault Systèmes progressed in these early stages, and Frank became good friends with the CEO Bernard Charlès. Dassault Systèmes had transformed other industries with their technology, and Frank and Bernard shared a vision to advance the building industry through the application of digital tools. At the time, very few people in the architecture and construction world were using 3D technology in their work. In order to get the client, the consultants and the contractors to use the Master Model/

Gehry Partners,
8 Spruce Street,
New York City,
2011

Seven sides of this 76-storey
mixed-use tower have an
undulating configuration, while
the south side is a flat plane.
The facade is constructed with
10,500 unique panels. Gehry
Partners and Gehry Technologies
worked closely with the
fabricator Permasteelisa on an
iterative automated design-
to-fabrication process. This
allowed the undulating building
envelope to be tuned to cost-
optimising constraints provided
by Permasteelisa, enabling its
delivery without change orders
and within a budget typical of
New York tower glass envelopes.

Gehry Technologies,
The Gehry Technologies and
Gehry Partners Ecosystem,
2002

below: The Gehry Technologies business was
founded with a mission to expand industry
capabilities supporting Gehry Partners projects,
while organising an ecosystem of technology
and professional partnerships.

Digital Delivery process, Gehry Partners had to take
on more responsibility across the team in order to
make the software and the approach work. They had to
help companies buy and install the technology; train
operators; and manage the workflow for all parties.
Around this time, Gehry Partners also started doing
quite a bit of research into developing the digital
delivery approach, producing supporting software and
developing new techniques to take advantage of all that
the technology could do. Dassault Systèmes was excited
about these developments and believed that Gehry
Partners was developing a revolutionary process for
architecture and construction.

Creating a Think-Tank

In 2002, CATIA Version 5 came out on Windows®
computers, and this represented a new set of
possibilities for the software, the industry and the firm.
The possibility that other firms could more easily acquire
the software, and the approach be used more broadly,
had a lot of appeal. Increasing the capabilities in the
industry could expand the pool for available partners,
expanding supply and therefore driving down cost.

It was into this environment that Gehry Technologies
(GT) was formed in 2002. For the original founders of
Gehry Technologies that came from the Gehry Partners
leadership, the technology company was about
promoting a new way of working that could restore
the Master Builder style of delivering projects back to
the mainstream. Frank had watched the architecture
profession change over the years. Architects had ceded
certain responsibilities on projects, fearing the growing
liabilities inherent in the job. They had relinquished
control to others to the detriment of the architecture.
What he saw in the use of digital delivery in his own

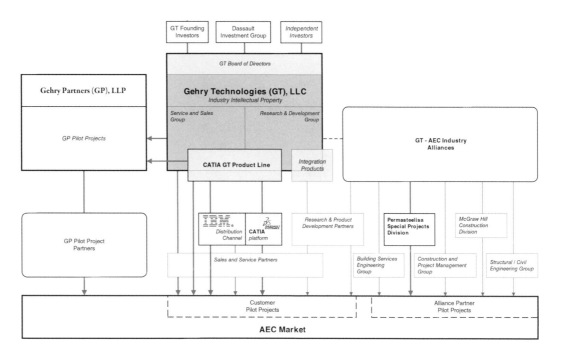

Gehry Technologies,
Lower Construction Command Center,
New York City,
2005

above: By using Digital Project connected to
scheduling software, Gehry Technologies provided
extensive 4D modelling capabilities to the New York
City agencies responsible for coordinating post-9/11
construction activities in lower Manhattan.

Gehry Technologies,
GTX Global Exchange,
2007

opposite: A cloud-based building information modelling (BIM) and project collaboration technology,
GTX was initially developed as a proof of concept by the design team of the Fondation Louis
Vuitton Museum in Paris (completed 2014) to manage collaborative work on the museum's model
by the globally distributed team. It combined model viewing, cloud services for processing
data and elements of social networking applied to the building project. GTX was subsequently
commercialised under the name GTEAM and became the basis for Trimble's Connect software.

The interest in digital delivery of projects was expanding in the industry, with building information modelling (BIM) becoming the prevalent terminology for the approach

projects was constructible clarity, which resulted in cost reduction and preservation of the design. Because of the clarity of the 3D data, he saw that the seemingly more complex ideas could be demystified. From the beginning, if something looked different, contractors would add a 'fear factor' to their pricing. This process eliminated the fear factor.

Gehry Technologies was created as an organisation to allow architects to take back the control of the process and to allow others to have the same successes in building that Gehry Partners enjoyed. Gehry Technologies would work to create new capabilities around the Master Model concept and tools, while increasing their adoption across the industry. Gehry Technologies would form an arm of the Gehry Partners ecosystem, augmenting the capacity of Gehry Partners through offerings and partnerships beyond the architectural practice. Gehry Partners would continue to drive innovation and opportunities on its projects, but Gehry Technologies' role was to industrialise these advances and use them to serve other building professionals as well. The costs of research and development could be borne by Gehry Technologies, and Gehry Technologies would help both the teams on Gehry Partners and other projects with buying, setting up, learning and using the software. Gehry Technologies took an investment from Dassault and started developing out a business model grounded in a partnership focused on the CATIA technology.

In 2004, the first commercial version of Gehry Technologies' software Digital Project was released, built on the engine of CATIA but with new capabilities targeted at the architectural design, contracting and fabricating communities. By 2008, Gehry Technologies was having success advancing the use of Digital Project and the Master Model approach across the globe. It turned out that changing to the Master Model approach was hard, and it took special projects and special leadership to make it happen. The interest in digital delivery of projects was expanding in the industry, with building information modelling (BIM) becoming the prevalent terminology for the approach. Gehry Technologies was increasingly brought in not just to help set up the software but to assist projects by providing modelling and information management services. By 2008, Gehry Technologies had 10 offices and 150 staff around the globe, and was working on many of the most visible projects in the world. The team was working with Zaha Hadid, Jean Nouvel, Skidmore Owings & Merrill and others. The global industry crash in 2008 affected the types of projects that used Digital Project and the Master Model, but there were new regions of the world and new types of projects that emerged. Gehry Technologies evolved to start working on infrastructure projects like the Mexico City and Hong Kong subway expansions and the World Trade Center redevelopment, as well as Disney's theme parks and other projects of complexity and scale. The Digital Project software was also increasingly used in academic programmes to teach aspects of parametric solid modelling.

Expanding the Mission

Gehry Technologies' business also started expanding beyond Digital Project. In 2007, one of Gehry Technologies' European directors began developing a new technology called GTX Global Exchange. This used the development and exchange of 3D models as the basis for a new way of working collaboratively over the internet. Gehry Technologies had been utilising source-control software used for collaborating on open-source software development as a means for sharing models across widely distributed projects. GTX put a web viewer on the model distribution software. It brought some of the ideas of social media into the idea of project organisation and communication. GTX worked with Digital Project but also with other software models. In 2010, Gehry Technologies organised a new round of investment – this time led by Autodesk – and started building out this new technology. The company started hiring people with skills in software products – product managers, developers, marketing and sales people.

The company also formed an advisory board of ten top architects and industry visionaries. This advisory board was intended to help provide direction to the company, not only in what capabilities were needed in the industry, but also to help maintain the ethos of the firm and its focus on assisting great designers to achieve great projects.

By 2013, the company had grown a lot. GTX had become GTEAM, and it was successfully being used as a cloud collaboration tool on Gehry Partners and Gehry Technologies projects. The company had grown past the original mission and Frank and the board of directors realised that it had perhaps outgrown the existing structure of the organisation.

In 2013 a chance meeting at the American Institute of Architects (AIA) National Convention with the leadership of the SketchUp® software provided a new direction. SketchUp had recently been acquired by Trimble – a large and growing AEC technology company with a vision to connect from design deep into the supply chain and onto the construction site, with software, spatial positioning and robotic technologies. Trimble had acquired a diverse set of companies and technologies and was interested in a web-connected approach to tying all of these capabilities together. Trimble's leadership also identified consulting as a needed piece of delivering their 'constructible model' approach to the industry. After many meetings, the leaders of the companies realised that they had not only a shared vision but also a shared culture. In 2014, Trimble acquired GTEAM and the consulting team.

In the five years since the acquisition, a lot has happened in Gehry Partners, Gehry Technologies and

Gehry Partners,
Luma Arles,
Arles, France,
due for completion 2020

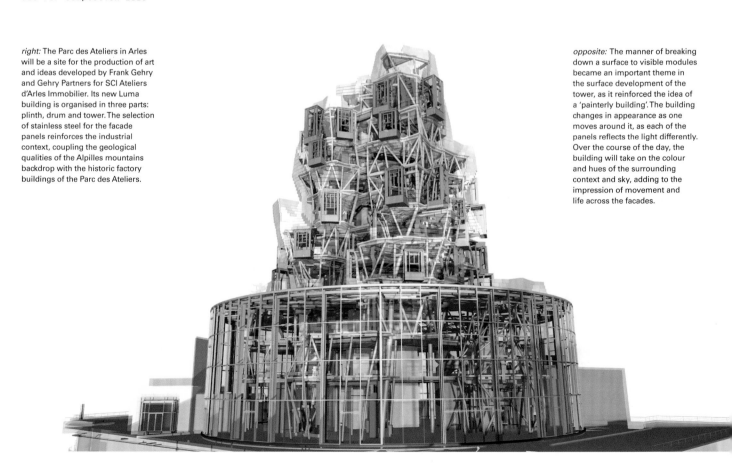

right: The Parc des Ateliers in Arles will be a site for the production of art and ideas developed by Frank Gehry and Gehry Partners for SCI Ateliers d'Arles Immobilier. Its new Luma building is organised in three parts: plinth, drum and tower. The selection of stainless steel for the facade panels reinforces the industrial context, coupling the geological qualities of the Alpilles mountains backdrop with the historic factory buildings of the Parc des Ateliers.

opposite: The manner of breaking down a surface to visible modules became an important theme in the surface development of the tower, as it reinforced the idea of a 'painterly building'. The building changes in appearance as one moves around it, as each of the panels reflects the light differently. Over the course of the day, the building will take on the colour and hues of the surrounding context and sky, adding to the impression of movement and life across the facades.

The original vision for Gehry Technologies of a think-tank of innovators both producing technologies and consulting across the industry resulted in a great portfolio of groundbreaking projects

the industry. GTEAM has been distributed internally across Trimble, with the software team becoming the basis for Trimble Connect. Now closely associated with SketchUp, the software has over five million users. The services team has become the basis for a new Trimble Consulting division. Gehry Partners continues to use Digital Project as a central part of its project delivery approach on current projects including the Luma Arles museum (due for completion in 2020). The Trimble services group continues to support Gehry Partners' projects, working both within the studio and outside on projects assisting contractors and fabricators in using the firm's models to deliver projects. Gehry Partners' partnership with Trimble has a new collaborative approach enabling projects including Gehry Partners' role in the masterplanning development for the Los Angeles River, which began in 2015 and is ongoing.

BIM of course continues to expand as an approach to delivering projects, although the promise of a fully integrated process driven by design into production remains to be broadly achieved in the industry. In many ways, the fragmentation of the industry disconnects and power struggles have been translated from traditional practice to the new tools. In some ways, the integrated Master Model approach realised on the early Gehry Partners projects is now farther away for the industry than it was then.

There are many lessons that can be drawn from the journey of Gehry Partners and Gehry Technologies, from its ambitions, struggles and successes. Gehry Technologies was formed at a particular moment in time in the industry when an opportunity and unfulfilled need was emerging around a paradigm shift in technology. The expanding need for 3D delivery at a time when the demand greatly exceeded the supply drove a lot of the expansion of the company. Gehry Technologies came into existence before the explosion of venture-funded disruptive tech companies that now attracts so much attention in the world, and access to investment and capital was not nearly as ubiquitous and formulaic as it is today.

The original vision for Gehry Technologies of a think-tank of innovators both producing technologies and consulting across the industry resulted in a great portfolio of groundbreaking projects, from concert halls and museums to subway systems and theme park rides. It built a generation of architectural tech innovators who have gone on to form new companies as well as lead the technical teams in both professional and software firms. It served and continues to serve as a vehicle for carrying the technology needs and processes of Gehry Partners' architectural partnership into its supply chain beyond the architecture firm's direct involvement. ⌀

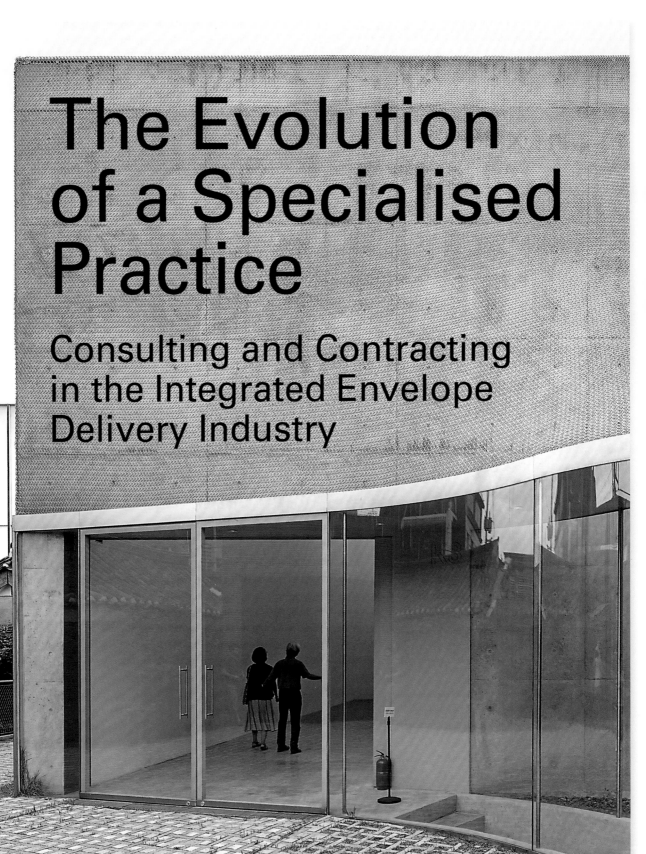

**Marc
Simmons**

The Evolution
of a Specialised
Practice

Consulting and Contracting
in the Integrated Envelope
Delivery Industry

In the last two decades the traditional relationship between architects and contractors has changed. Headquartered in Brooklyn, New York, Front, who specialise in building envelopes, have consistently blurred these supposed boundaries to achieve the high-performance facades on some of the most iconic architecture of these years. Front co-founder **Marc Simmons** explains these fluxing relationships and their holistic design benefits.

SO-IL,
Kukje Gallery K3,
Seoul,
2012

An award-winning project whose design is now part of the Museum of Modern Art in New York. It features a stark contrast between a pure Cartesian architectural concrete box and a fluid tensioned stainless-steel chainmail mesh. Working for SO-IL, Front developed project-specific digital tools to structurally analyse forces in the aggregated mesh rings while optimising the form-found geometry of the mesh. Front's affiliate Via sourced fabricators, oversaw the development of full-scale prototypes and served as turnkey supplier of the final assemblies.

Front is a building envelope design and consulting practice founded by architects, two of whom had met at Foster + Partners in the 1990s while working on the new Hong Kong Airport Ground Transportation Interchange (1998). The airport project introduced the founders at a young age and in a visceral way to the complexities of large-scale architectural and construction delivery. Working as an architect on a project of that scale and complexity enables an understanding of the roles of all the various consultants and contractors, and an appreciation of the role of specialist – in this case envelope – subcontractors. It becomes clear how much knowledge is present in the realms of specialisation on both the consultant and contracting side. The partners became interested in going deeper into this field of facades and building envelope. This interest became the catalyst for the formation of Front: a desire to understand everything happening around a specific specialism, to be a part of it, and then to own a greater part of the project in a specific specialisation.

From its inception, it was clear the practice would have a multidisciplinary skill set in order to deliver facade consulting and engineering. These skills included not just architectural design and drawing, but structural design, environmental design, means and methods, procurement, logistics, cost estimating, and also the kind of modelling and digital fabrication technologies that now underpin the workflows of the entire industry.

The opportunities for facade consultants proved to be very global with project locations, clients, architects, consultants, contractors and fabricators distributed across continents. This served as a catalyst for Front to expand out of New York to London, San Francisco and Hong Kong, servicing projects across global regions and facilitating local client workshops as well as factory, testing and site review visits. For many clients who operate internationally, they expect their consultants to have the same reach, benefiting equally from local and international knowledge, broad experience and best practices.

There is a great spectrum of companies working in facades, and a great number of associated personal motivations that drive and structure those distinct companies. Within the industry many are engineering oriented while others come to the discipline from architectural, environmental design and fabrication backgrounds. Front started in 2002 in a post-post-modernist world when all architectural idioms were up for grabs and technology was transforming industry through interoperability and an emerging participatory Web 2.0 socially networked culture. A central position of the firm relative to the work it takes on is that pluralism culturally and as manifest in the built environment is a good thing. Front experienced this working with architects on projects as diverse as SANAA's Grace Farms (New Canaan, Connecticut, 2015), OMA's China Central Television (Beijing, 2012) and Renzo Piano Building Workshop's Stavros Niarchos Foundation Cultural Center (Athens, 2016).

On any project, the goal of the firm is to engage collaboratively with that project's owner and the architectural team entrusted to deliver on the owner's aspirations. The first responsibility is to understand their goals and values, and the context in which they are applied, and then to help by any means it takes to realise the most ideal built incarnation of these ambitions. Front aspires to join the team prepared with an awareness of the client's body of work, its significance and how it may have been achieved technically and contractually.

Renzo Piano Building Workshop and Betaplan, Stavros Niarchos Foundation Cultural Center (SNFCC), Athens, 2016

The SNFCC incorporates monumental 24-metre-tall (79-foot) composite glass and steel walls with exterior motorised blinds, high-performance insulated cast-in-place concrete walls, a 10,000-square-metre (108,000-square-foot) photovoltaic array on the world's largest ferro-cement shell and various custom frameless glass walls and windows. Front provided facade consulting and engineering services throughout, representing the owners and the architects, and including the production of detailed drawings and technical specifications for the exterior envelope systems.

Crossing Over Into Contracting

By 2004, Front was hitting certain kinds of walls in the buoyant New York market. Ambitious projects of modest scale were either too small or too specialised to be of interest to qualified envelope contractors. Certain projects that Front had designed with the architect appeared possible to realise within budget, but not easily within what were then challenging market conditions. While design-assist by facade contractors was emerging as a way to manage a design-to-budget process, Front was intrigued by the opportunity to self-perform the works as a facade contractor moving from design consultant straight to design-build, not so much as a business opportunity but to enjoy the satisfaction of engaging all parts of project design and delivery.

Starting in 2004 the founding partners developed separate envelope delivery companies named Roxy and Via. In order to prevent any adverse impact to Front, these entities were never promoted and never engaged on a competitive basis with other facade contractors. They operated strictly on a private negotiated basis with clients who trusted Roxy and Via to self-perform its envelope designs, in turn employing Front with an expanded scope that included project management services, design, analysis and documentation of bespoke systems, the generation of shop drawings, assembly drawings, fab tickets as well as machine readable g-code. Roxy and Via would retain an independent engineer of record, and would subcontract material production, assembly and installation to companies qualified in these fields. Projects that had special qualities like Neil Denari's High Line 23 (New York, 2009) and CetraRuddy's Lincoln Square Synagogue (New York, 2013) would not have been realised in the manner designed had Front, through Roxy and Via, not stepped in and offered to deliver the systems at a budget-compliant cost in a way that the market was not able to provide at the time. There was an excitement in the firm about the possibility of doing total design and fully realising projects. Front, working for Roxy and Via, designed and managed 20 design-build projects over ten years in the background to its consulting business. Roxy and Via were viable businesses, had a great portfolio, and could have evolved into a full-scale design-build specialist contracting business. Some in the firm also articulated an opportunity to turn the building information modelling (BIM) skills, software tools and automation capabilities into a bona fide business. But ultimately Front is a closely held business with a few partners, whose hearts remain in collaborating on great architecture through design and process innovation in the consulting realm and not through contracting or technology product sales.

CetraRuddy,
Lincoln Square Synagogue,
New York City,
2013

above: An unprecedented undulating semi-unitised aluminium, steel and glass wall manifests as a metaphor for the five scrolls of the Torah. The glass panels feature laminated synthetic bronze fabric by Hermès's Créations Métaphores. The facade is further defined by custom integrated illumination, winning the IALD Radiance Award 2016. Front served as facade consultant to the architect, later handing over to affiliate Roxy Lab for complete system and lighting design integration, engineering, testing, fabrication and installation as managed by Front.

Neil M Denari Architects,
High Line 23 (HL23),
West Chelsea,
New York City,
2009

left: Defining the next generation of buildings along Chelsea's High Line, Neil Denari's HL23, cantilevering over the new elevated park, is a tour de force of geometrically stylised steel and glass. Front provided facade consulting services throughout for the complete enclosure while affiliate Via delivered full detailed design and fabrication produced in Shenzhen, as well as logistics planning and delivery of the glazing systems to site.

And Pulling Back

Front ultimately wound down Roxy and Via, pulling out of the contracting business and instead leveraged all of the knowledge that had been acquired – in logistics, scheduling, costs, procurement, means and methods, and detailed systems design, analysis, automation and quality control – emerging as an augmented and comprehensive building envelope design, engineering and consulting practice. This enhanced skill set, developed outside of the activities of traditional owner-side consulting, was certainly accelerated through the assumption of risk taken on by self-performing non-traditional design-build projects.

Through Front's design-build experience various digital tools were utilised and developed to manage a complete process from concept system design through to production, factory assembly, logistics and site installation sequencing. Elefront – a Rhinoceros®-based plugin that Front developed and now provides to the industry as free software – is one of these technologies. The Barclays Arena project (AECOM and SHoP, Brooklyn, New York, 2012), on which Front provided system design, analysis, shop drawings and fabrication tickets for the facade contractor in a predominantly CATIA / Digital Project environment, was the catalyst for evaluating the potential of creating similar capabilities in the Rhino® and Grasshopper® plugin world. Elefront is a key part of the firm's process for iterative design and analysis. It allows the essence of the proposed system, its variants and sub-variants to be captured. Once the design is set, this associative rule-based logic needs to be fully resolved into an ordered geometry to be deployed as shop drawing, assembly drawings, fab tickets and machine-specific G-code. Elefront allows attributes on digital facade objects to be retained at scale and detail and across the project supply chain. From these attributes, spreadsheets are created and interrogative overlays of spreadsheet data subsets are used to create input to structural and environmental analysis software as well as automated drawings through the use of project-specific document templates. Examples of projects benefiting from this workflow include Zaha Hadid's Morpheus Hotel (Macau, 2018) and TEN Arquitectos' Brooklyn Academy of Music (BAM) South project (Brooklyn, New York, 2018).

Since the firm's inception in 2002, the partners have developed full capabilities on both the consulting and contracting sides of projects. Front's partners' group of companies have included an architectural and engineering practice, general consulting companies by geographical region, a special inspection agency, and formerly product supply companies. This is a complex overhead just to enable operations for a small group of 40, but is needed to operate and compete across the global envelope markets and supply chains.

In part because of the capabilities gained from its facade design-build experience, Front now thrives in various alternative project-delivery environments. This has included prescriptive design and supply arrangements as deployed for the Kukje Gallery in Seoul by SO-IL (2012), builder-led design-build collaborations with architects and consultants under the general contractor such as The Century Project at the Seattle Space Needle by Olson Kundig (2018), working in IPD (integrated project delivery) contract projects such as Brown University's Center for Experimental Arts with RE X (Providence, Rhode Island, in construction), in collaborative design-assist projects as was required for the 5 Manhattan West repositioning by RE X (New York City, 2017) and classic design-bid-build but with augmented highly detailed drawing and BIM while deploying extensive pre-bid trial assemblies and prototypes as was done for both Renzo Piano's aforementioned Stavros Niarchos Foundation Cultural Center and the Canadian Parliament House of Commons at West Block in Ottawa, Canada (Architecture 49 and EVOQ Architecture, 2018). Working within these increasingly common project-delivery approaches, Front's scope of work is often more detailed than when working for the architect's team where they are naturally constrained to the scope of work assigned to architectural practices. Architect-led consultancy however remains the norm for Front's work and continues to represent the majority of Front's business, and the firm continues to find many opportunities for innovative approaches to system design, procurement and project delivery within normative projects such as 2050 M Street for developer Tishman Speyer with RE X and Kendall/Heaton Associates in Washington DC (2019).

Olson Kundig
Architects,
The Century Project
at the Seattle
Space Needle,
Seattle, Washington,
2018

This project involved the complete rehabilitation of the primary structure and the full reconstruction of all design surfaces within the top of the tower. Front worked for Olson Kundig, the architects, during the design stages, with a follow-on contract working for Hoffman Construction, the general contractor. The project did not have a traditional facade contractor; instead Front produced fully detailed and engineered systems based on existing structural survey data and delivered procurement packages for all components of the glass and metal systems.

TEN Arquitectos and Ismael Leyva Architects,
Brooklyn Academy of Music (BAM) South Tower,
Brooklyn, New York City,
2018

left: BAM South is a mixed-income 80/20 affordable housing rental project on a keystone site in Brooklyn. Front initially served as consultant to the developer Two Trees, resolving overall system detailing and meta-geometry, and was then novated to the fabricator Eastern Exterior Wall Systems, contracted to prepare complete panel and component geometry, assembly drawings, fabrication tickets and machine-readable G-code for several material systems.

RE X and Adamson Associates,
5 Manhattan West at Brookfield Place,
New York City,
2017

above: At 1.7 million square feet (160,000 square metres), 5 Manhattan West is the largest completed repositioning project in New York City. The entire building envelope was completely removed and re-clad with an iconic high-performance folded curtain wall, while the building was occupied. Front served as facade consultant through all work stages, representing the owner and architects and providing complete bid package drawings and specifications.

Architecture 49 and
EVOQ Architecture,
Canadian Parliament House
of Commons at West Block,
Parliament Hill,
Ottawa,
2018

Inaugurated in autumn 2018 for its
first session of Parliament serving as
the new House of Commons for the
government of Canada, the project
includes a self-structured steel and
glass infill to the existing courtyard
of West Block, the oldest building in
the parliamentary complex, having
been completed in 1865. The project
was executed on a design-bid-build
basis using coordinated construction
documents and extensive pre-bid
building information modelling (BIM).

RE X and Kendall/
Heaton Associates,
2050 M Street,
Washington DC,
2019

This 11-storey, 34,000-square-metre
(364,000-square-foot) freestanding
office development in the heart of
Washington DC's central business
district boasts one of the city's most
unique glass facades. Columns
located 3.7 metres (12 feet) inwards
of the floor-to-ceiling curved glass
curtain wall obviate the need for
vertical supporting mullions, enabling
unobstructed exterior views and
efficient build-out of perimeter offices.

Opportunities, Capabilities and Values

Building envelope has become of ever increasing importance as part of the broader building industry. It is currently a growth market, with this growth driven by many forces. One is simply the organic growth of the global population. Every year the world adds a rough approximation of 1 per cent new construction to the built environment while renovating an estimated 3 per cent of existing built fabric. That renovation work includes new additions and building performance upgrades. Today Front's portfolio by project count includes one-third adaptive reuse work including re-clads, additions, insertions and renovations to existing structures.

A second major factor is climate change and its responses. General requirements for environmental performance have improved incrementally and sometimes dramatically. These are very positive forces that will compel appropriate and needed investments in the building envelope and overall building performance.

The envelope today, as it has performed through history, is a true threshold, not just for environment, shelter and privacy but importantly for physical security. Many of Front's projects have security performance overlays onto the building envelope, with threat assessment and mitigation defined by owners and specialist advisers.

A third factor is the undeniable role of envelope as cultural signifier, as brand and as media vehicle. The creation and reinforcement of identity or brand through form and materiality, integrated graphics, signage, lighting and physical-digital media is profound and informs the evaluation, design, procurement and operational considerations for every project today.

These factors are all emerging value-creation forces in the industry and increase the challenge for successful project realisation when budget and schedule remain essential constraints. Delivering against these forces is a huge challenge for the construction industry: there are very few contractors worldwide that really have the requisite skill set. So as a consulting practice Front has had the opportunity and the necessity to step up to handle this work in a myriad of collaborative, contractual and project-delivery structures.

The forward-looking challenges facing the built environment are not unknown: they are front and centre, and concern climate change and social equity. These are issues that go way beyond facade engineering, but these forces and the resulting market demands are creating opportunities for the firm to contribute to new kinds of projects such as those in the civic, utility and infrastructure realms as well as with education and affordable and mixed-income housing work. Front has also engaged in pro-bono work, community engagement activities and projects through teaching in academic institutions focusing on design addressing the needs of unaccompanied minors. Recognising that the climate crisis, as a real and significant catalyst for involuntary human displacement, and the refugee-migrant crisis are inextricably linked, it places even sharper focus on the need for urban planning and building design to mitigate climate change while contributing to enhanced social equity. In response, through the partner's work in the School of Architecture and Planning at the Massachusetts Institute of Technology (MIT), Front has developed a cooperative relationship with the Home Project: a nonprofit that builds and operates shelters for unaccompanied refugee minors. For the past two years, Front, through design studios at MIT, has been working with the Home Project to analyse and improve the Home Project's shelters, a collection of 11 traditional concrete-framed buildings in central Athens. This collaboration resulted in both incremental improvements to existing shelters and a rooftop urban-agriculture food garden classroom prototype built by students and volunteers for one of the shelters. The Home Project with World Wildlife Fund Greece and the Athens Partnership are now implementing a pedagogical programme to teach urban agricultural skills to children.

Front's evolution as a firm and the skill set gained through this evolution are what enable it to now take on these sorts of projects. As a global consulting practice, this capacity starts with a holistic understanding of the kinds of problems of envelopes, identification of needs, the ability to build relationships and to create the circumstances under which one can actually act, and ultimately to carry a project to realisation. Whether it is a public library in Seattle, a sanitation garage in Manhattan, an affordable housing project in the Bronx, or a rooftop agriculture classroom in Athens, eventually the same skill set can be deployed predicated on collaborative team and relationship building. This is a significant direction for the firm now: applying the skill set Front has accumulated to enhancing the experience and quality of life for a greater number of people, be it through commissioned, pro-bono or academic engagements. ⌂

The forward-looking challenges facing the built environment are not unknown: they are front and centre, and concern climate change and social equity

Text © 2020 John Wiley & Sons Ltd. Images: pp 24–6, 30(b) © Front Inc, photo Marc Simmons; p 27 © Front Inc, photo Jill Fredrickson; pp 28, 29(b) © Front Inc, photo Miguel Otero Fuentes; p 29(t) © Front Inc, photo Richard Green; p 30(t) © Front Inc, photo Patrick Deveau

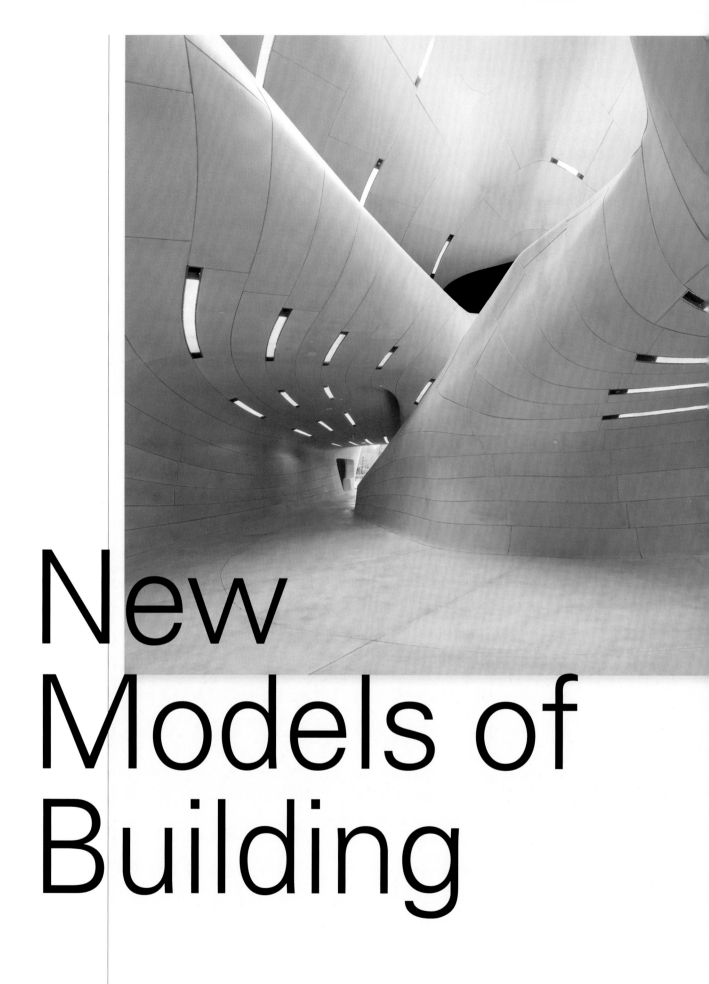

New Models of Building

Architects' interest in new technology is often focused on its ability to create new shapes for their buildings. But technology offers opportunities of differing funding models that both use architects' skills and create new ways for them to be paid. **David Fano and Daniel Davis** illustrate these opportunities using their experiences with the New York–based consultancy CASE and the international workspace enterprise WeWork.

The Business of Technology

For all the things technology has changed about our profession, the business model is not one of them: architects still trade time for money; schools still insist that accreditation is the path to success.

When architects talk about digital transformation, they typically talk about parametric models, curvaceous facades, building information modelling (BIM) standards, digital twins and virtual reality. They talk about technology transforming how they work. But they do not normally talk about technology transforming how they get paid. They spend inordinate amounts of time discussing whether parametric design justifies the enunciation of a new architectural style, they spend hours upon hours reinventing panelling algorithms for towers in cities they will never visit, and they debate, endlessly, how to improve BIM standards instead of discussing how to improve design standards. They often assume that new innovations will flow into the industry and that they will keep doing what they do – business as usual with quicker computers and newer software.

As the industry stands still, a number of companies with non-traditional business models are entering the market and hoping to take a slice of the US$10 trillion global construction industry.[1] There are established tech companies (Google, Tesla, Airbnb, Amazon), well-funded vertically integrated organisations (WeWork and Katerra), and a whole host of prefabrication startups and software ventures. These companies represent a dramatic investment in new business models. By one estimate, US$10 billion was invested in prop-tech startups in 2018.[2] To put that figure in perspective, the entire US architectural services industry was worth about US$45 billion in 2018.[3]

These new ventures pose an existential threat to the architecture industry since they are not beholden to the industry's established structures. But at the same time, these ventures present opportunities for architects to pursue non-traditional careers and for architecture firms to develop non-traditional business models. And so, as architects come to terms with technology transforming how they work, they should also ask how it can transform their business.

A New Model, a New Business
Founded in 2008, CASE Inc was a consultancy that helped firms transform their business through technology. Its three founders had all come from SHoP Architects, an entrepreneurial firm that has deviated from the traditional business of architecture to start its own construction company (SHoP Construction), spin out a real-estate startup (Envolope) and, on some projects, opt for payment in equity rather than fees.[4]

WhoByYou, Homepage, 2010

WhoByYou was an early attempt at moving from an architecture firm into an adjacent industry. Although it was not commercially successful, the team that made WhoByYou would go on to create CASE Inc, a consultancy that would later become integral to WeWork.

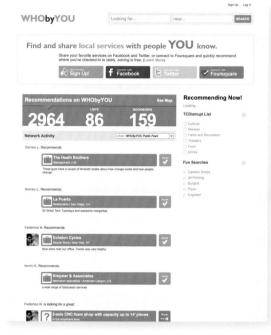

Initially CASE's consultancy services were a side-business, a way to pay the bills while they launched a startup called WhoByYou. The latter, their main focus, was a website where people could share and recommend service providers (such as architects and builders), making it easier to discover local businesses. Within a couple of years it became apparent that there was more demand for the consultancy business than for WhoByYou, and by 2011 development on the startup ceased.

On the consulting side, the breakthrough project for CASE was the Louisiana Sports Hall of Fame by Trahan Architects (2013). The interior was made of 1,150 uniquely curved stone panels and CASE were entrusted to develop the panels' fabrication drawings and to coordinate all the services that interfaced with them. This project was by far the largest and most complex that CASE had undertaken.

CASE continued to work with a variety of firms in the AEC industry, helping them gain a technological edge through training, software development and strategic planning. Despite the success of this work, CASE were ultimately limited by the amount of control their clients had over the design and construction process. For example, CASE could promote model-based delivery, but unless the contractor, owner and municipality were set up to take the models (inevitably they were not), their client still had to produce paper drawing sets. Or CASE could talk about efficiency improvements with their clients, but since most clients were charging for labour it was a hard sell financially. In the end, CASE never saw the advancement that they hoped for, since everything was happening in this fragmented ecosystem where very few, if any, of the players actually benefited from improving the process.

So Who Tends To Work Together?

CASE,
Location
Dashboard,
2015

Using location data, CASE were able to infer who spent time working together and how particular sub-teams interacted. This spatial data gave insight into the organisational dynamics that were not apparent just from looking at the organisational chart.

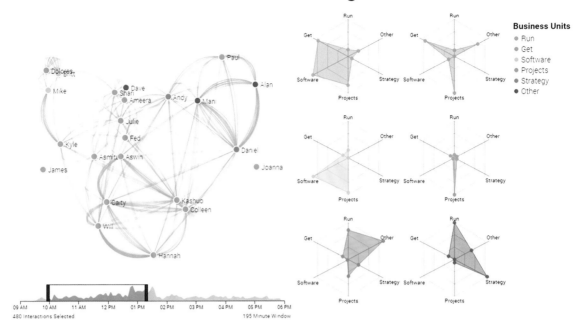

Business Units
- Run
- Get
- Software
- Projects
- Strategy
- Other

CASE,
SOM BIM Dashboard,
2012

The experience of creating WhoByYou provided a foundation from which CASE Inc developed a number of custom web applications for clients. The paper prototype depicts a dashboard that CASE were developing for the international architecture and urbanism practice Skidmore, Owings & Merrill (SOM).

The completed dashboard allowed people at SOM to track the progress of active projects across the firm. Typically project data is only relevant to that project but CASE were able to demonstrate that aggregating this data tells a much larger story about the health of a business.

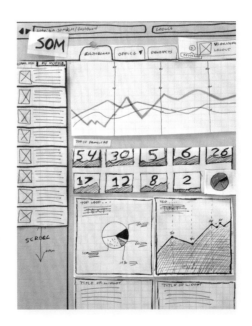

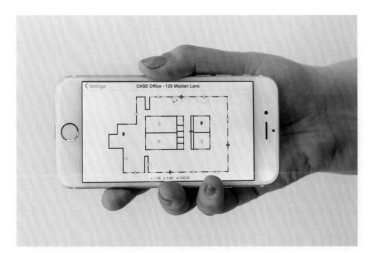

CASE,
Location Tracker App,
2015

Prior to being acquired by WeWork, CASE Inc were studying how buildings could be evaluated using location data. The app they developed tracked the location of a person in an office using Bluetooth beacons.

 Bldg Analytics   Search for projects... 🔍   👤 ⚙ →]

Project Portfolio

Project Map

● Active ● Complete

🕐 Project GSF ▾   🗺 ☰

Projects by City

34

■ New York (35%)   **12**
■ San Francisco (32%)   **11**
■ Chicago (18%)   **6**
■ All Others (15%)   **5**

Portfolio Square Footage
Running Total

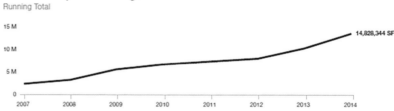

14,828,344 SF

Active Project Schedule

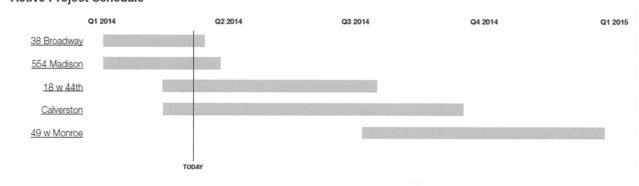

	Q1 2014	Q2 2014	Q3 2014	Q4 2014	Q1 2015
38 Broadway					
554 Madison					
18 w 44th					
Calverston					
49 w Monroe					

TODAY

List of All Projects

CASE,
Building Portfolio Dashboard,
2015

Building on the work of the SOM Dashboard, CASE developed a tool for
understanding the sequencing of real-estate deals and construction. When
CASE was acquired by WeWork, this technology became integral to how
WeWork planned its global expansion.

CASE tried to combat this institutional inertia by moving up the food chain to work with more building owners. This is a strategy that other companies, such as Autodesk, have successfully deployed to force innovations like BIM onto the supply chain. One of these owners, WeWork, were a startup the CASE founders met while starting WhoByYou. At that time, WeWork were still a young company using vertical integration to create workspaces around the world (doing real estate, design, construction, sales and facilities management in-house). As WeWork grew, it quickly became CASE's largest client. Eventually, CASE's founders decided to go all-in and see what would happen if they took this technology and applied it to a new business model rather than forcing it onto the old model. So CASE took a seat on the other side of the table and joined WeWork.

What Really Matters

It has been something of a revelation to work as a building owner. From the other side it becomes clear that architects often pursue technology as an end in itself while losing sight of the larger objectives. In particular, there are four areas of practice that seem especially overlooked by architects, technologists and academics – areas of practice that should be the focus of future endeavours. Explored in the following paragraphs, they are: user experience; feedback; the higher purpose; and the ancillary aspects of the business.

First, user experience. Architects win work well before any design or construction has started. Early on, the architect needs to convince the client that their vision of the future is worth building, whether through a competition, a bid or just a lot of charm. In these early phases, it is difficult to sell the feeling of inhabiting a project because experiences are hard to convey without being there. So architects rely on the project's visual iconography to make the sale. As a result, an inordinate amount of time, resources and technology goes into creating unique, visually appealing forms. Some of the best minds in the industry have been squandered working out how to transfer this strange geometry from one software to the next. And the tragedy is that people do not experience buildings from the outside. So this obsession with the exterior offers no benefit to the occupants (if anything, it makes construction and the resulting space more expensive).

Architects need to take the lived, inhabited experience more seriously. All these resources they waste on iconic facades should be focused inwards. Technology could be used to sell experiences rather than forms. If nothing else, they should give more respect to interiors. Even within the architectural curriculum, interiors tend to be an overlooked subject, with overt sexism (by one estimate, 87 per cent of interior designers are women[5]), and is often degraded as pillows and wall coverings. This has to change. Architects have to truly add value and make the experience better. The interior experience trumps curving facades.

Then there is the matter of feedback. Most architects do not know what happens behind the walls they

build. A small number of firms conduct regular post-occupancy evaluations, but even this tends to be fairly cursory, typically only occurring once in the lifetime of a building. For most architects, advancing the occupant experience is impossible because they do not know the baseline experience.

Simply put, architects do not spend enough time researching their end-users. And the little research that does occur, tends to be in service of marketing rather than occupants. But savvy clients are beginning to ask for more performative data. It is another area of practice that technologists have neglected, with post-occupancy studies relying on techniques that were in use decades ago (namely surveys and observational studies). There is significant potential to put more resources into studying how people use spaces, creating predictive models of how spaces will perform, and using technology to truly understand and improve people's lives.

Third, there is the need to focus on the project's higher purpose – prioritising the end over the means. Over the past decade, much of technology discourse has been dominated by devout debates about methods and implementations. The UK BIM mandates, the COBie (construction operations building information exchange) data format, the role of the BIM manager, integrated project delivery (IPD) contracts and the best way to deal with interoperability. In all of this, the larger objective has been lost amongst the tactical handwringing. So you have a clash-free building; now what?

To be clear, clashes certainly are not desirable, but clash avoidance is not why architects get out of bed every day. The higher purpose has been lost to these smaller pragmatic challenges. Rather than starting with how to do something, architects should be starting with why. Once the objective is in place there can be a debate about how to achieve the outcome. This might involve using a standard like the Industry Foundation Classes (IFC) data model, but it might also require going astray, as WeWork often did, and forging your own path. The objective should not be to deliver perfectly compliant IFC models; it should be to create better environments.

Lastly, there are the non-design-related aspects of the practice. Taken as a whole, technology is often applied to a relatively narrow area of an architecture firm. A firm might have people that specialise in using computation to help with difficult geometric problems or BIM operability, but the same enthusiasm is rarely shown for knowledge management, human resources, marketing, research and so forth.

These aspects of the business perhaps seem ancillary to the serious duty of designing buildings, but they are still important. At WeWork, for instance, analysis of design feedback showed that if the base building was bad (poor light, bad services), it did not matter how well the office was designed, the flaws in the base building would spoil the experience. So picking real estate was actually a key design choice, one that merited investment of a lot of technological resources. In a similar vein, there is a lot of scope to apply computational innovations to the rest of an architecture firm.

Getting Paid

Nicholas Negroponte ends his seminal book *The Architectural Machine* (1970) with a warning:

> Many computer aided design studies are relevant only insofar as they present more fashionable and faster ways of doing what designers already do. And since what designers already do doesn't seem to work, we get inbred methods that make bad architecture, unresponsive architecture, even more prolific.[6]

Negroponte's entire book is prophetic, overflowing with early prototypes of many technologies we talk about as breathless innovations today – virtual reality, generative design, voice assistants, machine learning and so on. But his warning seems to have been lost with time. In the 50 years since Negroponte published his book, technology has made some processes faster and offered more fashionable ways of working, but at a fundamental level, not a lot has changed.

With many architecture firms working to apply new technology to an old model, a number of companies outside the industry have entered the market with new ways of funding design. A huge market is opening up for prop-tech (technology related to real estate), which is why technology companies like Google are starting development arms (Sidewalk Labs). There are a number of interesting fields emerging: prefabrication startups (FullStack Modular, Kasita and Blokable), furniture supply-chain software (Clippings), off-market development opportunities (Envelope) and early-stage test-fit software (TestFit, Spacemaker and ArchiStar).

In many ways, architecture firms are perfectly positioned to go after these emerging markets – they already have the creative skills, the domain expertise and the industry connections. Obviously there are some challenges in switching from selling services to selling products, but these are surmountable. Already we are seeing firms experimenting in this space. Thornton Tomasetti partnered with venture capitalists to launch an incubator, TTWiiN; UNStudio spun out UNSense, a startup for sensing the built environment; and Kieran Timberlake have begun selling some of their internal tools. While it is still early days for all these ventures, these firms are showing that technology is not just transforming how we work but also providing opportunities to rethink the business altogether.

These new business models can sound ominous since they represent disruptions to the status quo, but they also present opportunities. If nothing else, they demonstrate that there is demand for new business models, money available to fund new ventures, and an appetite for experimentation. Rather than spending time lamenting a lost profession, it should be the responsibility of architects to take the lead, to learn from other design and technology fields, and to morph architecture into what it needs to be.

There is a long history of architects setting out and succeeding in other fields. In recent years, architects have left the profession to found some of the biggest technology companies. Miguel McKelvey worked as an architect before co-founding WeWork; Evan Sharp studied at the Columbia Graduate School of Architecture, Planning and Preservation (GSAPP) before co-founding Pinterest; and Brian Chesky and Joe Gebbia, the co-founders of Airbnb, met at the Rhode Island School of Design. And for every one of these figureheads, there are countless others who left architecture to become successful programmers, strategists, UX designers and on and on.

While this could represent something of a brain drain in the industry, it speaks of the strength of the architectural education. People coming out of architecture school have been taught to challenge everything, craft thoughtful solutions and communicate clearly. It is a wonderful education that prepares people for many of the challenges in the modern economy. But architecture schools are typically only focused on graduating students that will go on to become registered architects, so these alternative pathways are frequently hidden from view. Given this drive for accreditation, leaving the profession is often seen as a failure of the industry when really it is a demonstration of strength, a sign of the growing importance of design in other businesses. Architecture schools should be harnessing these alternative opportunities to better the world through design, and students should not be afraid to step outside the bounds of a 'normal' career, at least long enough to pay off their loans, because the world needs the expertise of architects, even if it does not come from a traditional architecture firm.

WeWork, Corrigan Station, Kansas City, Missouri, 2018

At WeWork, an in-house team manages the sourcing, design, construction and operations of every office. This vertically integrated approach has challenged many incumbents who are operating in a more fractured delivery system, allowing WeWork to expand rapidly in the past 10 years.

Notes
1. McKinsey & Company, *Reinventing Construction: A Route To Higher Productivity*, whitepaper, 2017, p vi.
2. CREtech, *2018 End of Year Report*, whitepaper, 2018.
3. AIA, *Firm Survey Report 2018: Business of Architecture*, whitepaper, 2018.
4. Andrew Rice, 'From Barclays Center To Modular High Rises, SHoP Architects Is Changing The Way We Build Buildings', *FastCompany*, 10 February 2014: www.fastcompany.com/3025601/shop-architects-the-new-skyline.
5. 'Interior Designer Demographics in the United States', CareerExplorer, 2019: www.careerexplorer.com/careers/interior-designer/demographics/.
6. Nicholas Negroponte, *The Architectural Machine*, MIT Press (Cambridge, MA), 1970, p 121.

Helen Castle

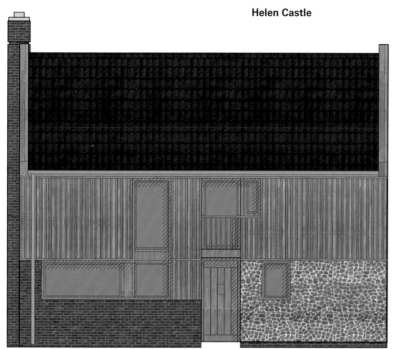
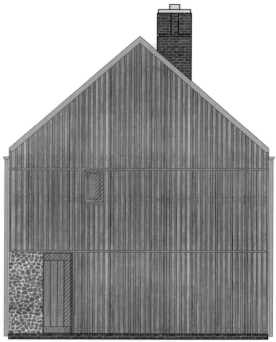

Disrupting from

Project Orange,
Elevation option selection for House Type A1,
Ingoldisthorpe, Norfolk,
2019

The creation of a design code allows for both variety and consistency in housing types. The developed vocabulary and use of materials are in keeping with the local vernacular. This is expressed in a palette that includes pantile, red brick, stained timber and Carr stone.

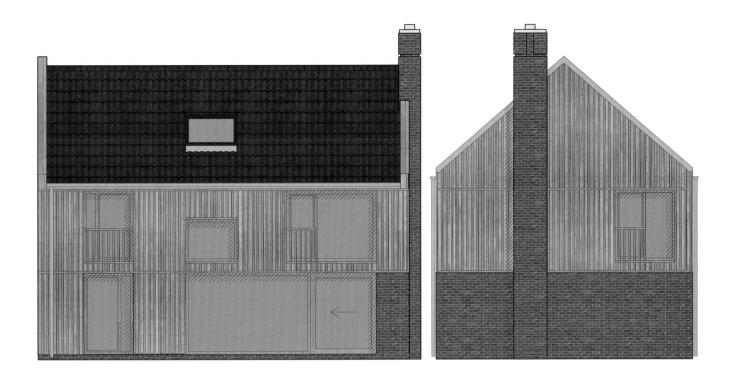

the Inside
UK Archipreneurs

No longer restricted to designing buildings, architectural practices are seizing the opportunity to diversify. They are redefining the architect's role by embracing a wide variety of relationships up and down the design and construction procurement chain, utilising new technologies for digital fabrication, development economics and building performance analysis, as well as advising clients on their business models. RIBA Publishing Director **Helen Castle,** former Editor of $\triangle$, describes how this shift is panning out in the UK.

In the UK, an evolution is underway. A highly pragmatic and savvy generation of architects is spearheading a step-change in the design and construction industry. Located in established practices, they are transforming architecture from the inside out. Working for themselves or in senior positions, they are less interested in the formulation of their studio's design brand than in developing techniques and processes that tackle current limitations, creating better-value propositions for their clients. There is a consensus that the existing professional services model that relies on architects' billable hours, confined to the conventional design and delivery stages of traditional procurement routes, is no longer sustainable for the profession. Intent on clawing back the territory lost to project managers and large contractors over the last few decades, they are developing new types of services at RIBA Stages 0 and 7 and shaping automated design and construction techniques in-between. This is most often manifesting itself in strategic and business services prior to design phase, design for manufacture and assembly (DfMA) consultancy work and post-occupancy services after completion.

This shift is not just confined to the large international offices; bright spots of innovation are popping up in small regional studios. To establish the full spectrum and impact of this significant shift, interviews were undertaken with four practitioners working at different levels and scales, and both inside and outside London: Jaimie Johnston of Bryden Wood; Tomas Millar of Millar + Howard Workshop; David Ayre of Ayre Chamberlain Gaunt; and Xavier De Kestelier of HASSELL. But how did we get here?

A High-Tech Lineage of Entrepreneurism
The notion of architecture as a commercial activity, which requires entrepreneurial shrewdness, is relatively recent. In the mid-20th century, most architects worked for the state or local authorities' architecture departments. In 1952–3, the London County Council Architects Department was the largest practice in the world with 1,577 staff.[1] By the early 1970s, half of UK architects still worked for the public sector.[2] By the late 1960s, though, architects were already starting to develop their own interest in producing a new type of architecture, serving commercial clients, before the plug was finally pulled on the public sector by the Thatcher government with the privatisation of housing and national industries in the 1980s. Sir Terry Farrell, who met his first practice partner, Sir Nicholas Grimshaw, as a fellow staff architect at the LCC in 1961, describes how he and his High-Tech peers in the late 1960s 'enthusiastically embraced the private sector', making 'a complete break from the current generation of leading practices that were almost solely reliant on the State and State-related cultures of the Welfare State'.[3] This freed them up to work with a new breed of clients and on a wider variety of building types, as they started designing commercial buildings, such as offices, warehouses and factories, and speculative housing for developers. Running their practices more like businesses, High-Tech architects were also pioneering in their understanding of the power of branding and application of marketing and publicity techniques.

The High-Tech practices also engendered an enthusiasm for the technical and an experimental use of design and construction systems, as described by Farrell: 'the link to construction and the design of building components was also part of this new attitude to private sector and entrepreneurial endeavour. Cladding, mechanical engineering, structural-steel systems and off-site component fabrication and part assembly got all of us into the industrial design of building elements and thoroughly engaged in doing so with the private sector construction industry.'[4] It was this interest in architecture as a commercial activity, underpinned by high design and innovative uses of technology, that was to have such an enduring impact on UK architectural culture. To this day, for instance, Foster + Partners and Grimshaw are recognised worldwide not only for the quality of their design work, but also for their technological expertise and capacity for technical innovation.

JAIMIE JOHNSTON

Bryden Wood

Bryden Wood has a direct line to the High-Tech with its interest in building components and the construction industry. Founding partners Mark Bryden and Martin Wood both left Grimshaw in 1995 to form the practice. There was by this time a sense that even for top practices, opportunities were diminishing for architects to lead on the construction process, material and detailing. As Jaimie Johnston, Director and Head of Global Systems at Bryden Wood, who has worked with the partners for over 24 years from its earliest beginnings, explains: 'Martin wanted to be an architect, but not in this industry. High-profile architecture was being delivered by blokes with a hammer and a white van.' This was just after the Latham Report of 1994, which identified systemic failings in the construction industry. As Johnston explains: 'There was the sense that there was about to be a shift and both partners were keen to capitalise on it.'

By working with the establishment, Bryden Wood has arguably single-handedly led a U-turn in design and construction in the UK. In 2018, it was the first architectural practice to be awarded the Queen's Enterprise Award for Innovation for its work leading the industry's adoption of off-site and advanced construction techniques. Furthermore, in 2019 its Creative Technologies Team beat off Foster + Partners and Grimshaw to win the AJ100 Best Use of Technology award. This specifically recognised its work in developing planning-compliant open-source web apps for the end users of primary schools, and systemised housing schemes and a rapid engineering model based on analysis of Highways England's technical guides to accelerate road infrastructure design for the Smart Motorways programme. Bryden Wood's clients include several major government departments – the Ministry of Justice, Highways England and the Education Skills Funding Agency – as well as corporates such as GlaxoSmithKline, Heathrow Airport and Circle Health.

Jaimie Johnston working with
a team at Bryden Wood,
London,
2019

At Bryden Wood, teams are integrated rather than multidisciplinary, taking in clients as well as engineers and members of staff with other skills such as business analytics, coding and app design.

Bryden Wood,
Circle Birmingham Hospital,
Birmingham,
2019

The building is the second hospital Bryden Wood has undertaken for health provider Circle Health. Clinical outcomes and construction efficiencies are optimised by building on the research and analysis that was undertaken for the practice's previous Circle Health hospital in Reading.

Johnston himself plays a pivotal role in influencing and informing government. He was a member of the UK Government BIM Task Force, chaired by Mark Bew, which drove the public sector's adoption of building information modelling (BIM) with the advocacy of Level 2 in 2016. He has written several reports for Digital Built Britain, a partnership between the Department for Business, Energy & Industrial Strategy and the University of Cambridge, which articulate the government's aspiration to adopt a more manufacturing-led approach to construction that will enable its transformation into a smart digital industry.[5] In December 2018, Johnston was appointed the Design Lead for the Construction Innovation Hub (CIH), which has been tasked with developing digital technologies and off-site manufacture, and granted £72 million by government via UK Innovate for its R&D work. Bryden Wood is leading on the creation of 'product family architectures' – standardised designs and components – for new buildings across the government estate. Working with key government departments, analysing building types for each, the intention is to enable them to deliver most of their buildings in this way. At Bryden Wood, Johnston has responsibility for both physical systems, such as design for manufacture and build solutions, and information systems, including data analysis, digital delivery and BIM.

From early on, Bryden Wood recognised that the main barriers to clients adopting DfMA systems were technical. To enable learning and problem solving, it was necessary to physically assemble and manufacture buildings. From 2004, for eight years, Bryden Wood owned its own factory, which was used for building the prefabricated components for the EcoCanopy primary schools project (2014), as well as prototyping systems for schools and hospitals. The factory facility has now shifted to a prototyping research centre, which enables the practice to 'develop cross-sector construction platforms – DfMA systems', which can be tested to 'measure the benefits in programme productivity and quality'.

Despite this focus on the refinement of the physical manufacturing process, Bryden Wood is 'very often not designing a building'. By 'relentlessly pursuing value for clients', its focus has now become more about work prior to the design phase, interrogating the brief and the business case. For every capital project that Bryden Wood is employed on for GlaxoSmithKline, they develop a problem statement. This requires data analytics and visualisations from the Creative Technologies team. It involves broad skills from the financial people and process engineering. To benefit clients further, the practice often insists that IP can be used for future projects or shared across government. As Johnston states: 'For repeat clients, design fees reduce after the first project (where all the learning is done)'. This enables Bryden Wood to create long-term relationships that allow them to work with their clients earlier in their projects and business processes. They create blended teams from the practice, the client side and external experts. To facilitate this close collaboration, many clients are co-located in their office, enabling faster communication. The emphasis is on the reciprocation of IP and sharing of solutions between clients, enabling everyone to 'benefit faster'.

Providing a holistic 'design for value' service for its clients, Bryden Wood has embraced the master builder model. They have moved the practice in the opposite direction to the dominant trend towards specialisation, accepting risk in an industry that has become risk adverse. They are in the position that they are addressing high-level exam questions for the government's Infrastructure and Projects Authority: How do you build 6 million homes? Or how do you house an additional prison population of 10,000 while investing them with skills? This sometimes results in them working as DfMA consultants alongside other architects. At a time that other UK practices are contracting or standing still, unnerved by the uncertainty of Brexit, Bryden Wood is continuing to grow. It is currently recruiting 20 new staff to an existing staff of 240, largely based in its Clerkenwell office in London, with subsidiaries in Singapore, Barcelona and St Albans. Almost half the staff are architects; 30 per cent are mechanical engineers; 20 per cent structural engineers; with other individuals with expertise in coding, apps and business analytics. It remains architect-led, however. In Johnston's words, 'optimising on architects' abilities to liaise with teams, clients and understand constraints'.

Bryden Wood,
Circle Birmingham Hospital,
Birmingham,
2019

The building is the second hospital Bryden Wood has undertaken for health provider Circle Health. Clinical outcomes and construction efficiencies are optimised by building on the research and analysis that was undertaken for the practice's previous Circle Health hospital in Reading.

From early on, Bryden Wood recognised that the main barriers to clients adopting DfMA systems were technical

TOMAS MILLAR

Millar + Howard Workshop

The Millar + Howard Workshop team at the St Mary's Mill studio, Stroud, Gloucestershire, 2019

The team on their coffee break outside the firm's studio. Second from the left, Tomas Millar, and second from the right, Tom Howard.

The Millar + Howard Workshop, in contrast, could not be located further away from London's tech hub in Shoreditch. Its studio is in Stroud, Gloucestershire, a 19th-century mill town nestled in the Cotswold Hills, which was once famous for Stroud Scarlet, the cloth that supplied the red coats of the British army. With a vibrant cafe culture, quirky independent shops and a canalside scattered with converted textile mills, Stroud has developed a distinct, arty identity out of its rich industrial past. It is home to one of the largest artistic communities outside London. Damien Hirst's Science Ltd studio is based there as well as Pangolin Editions, a large foundry that casts sculptures for artists internationally.

Like Bryden Wood, Tomas Millar and Tom Howard's innovations originate out of the frustrations of making architecture. Talented students, who initially studied together at Edinburgh, the two partners started out undertaking small design and build projects. While still completing Part 2 and Part 3 in London, they were constructing tree houses and garden rooms – dividing their year between winters in London and summers in Gloucestershire. Going to parties, meeting contemporaries, other people immediately 'got what they did'. Millar describes the way they were working as 'feeling right'. Ultimately, though, they found that when it came to bigger projects, specialist contractors were required. In 2008 they made the decision to focus solely on design, setting up a studio in their home town of Stroud.

By 2012, Millar + Howard Workshop was fully established. It was only when an employee asked about project management that Millar started reading up on the subject and engaging in business thinking. Millar and Howard realised that there were opportunities in Stroud for development, where there were both brownfield and greenfield sites available, and demand, with a wealthy catchment area of potential homebuyers in Gloucestershire. The practice was receiving similar repeat briefs for designing new-build homes: a ground floor with open-plan living, boot room, a snug and office, and three to four bedrooms. In 2014 they used the proceeds from Howard selling his own home and a larger pot of other people's investments to set up a separate development company, Livedin. One after the other they bought three sites and undertook the design of three or four houses on each, selling on each as individual plots with planning permission.

Millar + Howard Workshop, Dursley Treehouse, Gloucestershire, 2015

Designed to Passivhaus principles and to have minimal impact on the 27 protected trees surrounding the site, the treehouse was project-managed and constructed by the client. Featured in September 2016 on British television series 'Grand Designs', there has been significant public interest in this romantic, cantilevered structure with its veranda that extends out into the tree canopy.

In parallel, Millar was also developing virtual reality (VR) for the practice's domestic clients. It provided a clear technological solution for clients who were unable to visualise plans. It enabled homeowners to effectively see and experience their home before it was built. Like design and build, it once again brought clients closer to what they wanted.

As a passionate advocate of lean thinking,[6] which places an emphasis on what customers want and testing ideas through continuous adaptation of a minimum viable product, conventional practice continually makes less sense to Millar. Individual small practices, like Millar + Howard Workshop, throughout the country are repeating the same manual tasks hundreds of times over – generating floor plans and door schedules. The proverbial issue of difficult relationships with contractors remains an ongoing rub and barrier to efficient delivery of projects for architects and clients alike. There is a yearning on Millar's part for the design/build setup of the early years that made such clear sense as a proposition to all those involved.

The next venture for Millar and Howard lies in the evolution of their development arm Livedin, which has the potential to revolutionise rural domestic land development. The aspiration is that it will do for development what Airbnb has done for holiday rental. With the support of friend and long-term collaborator Charlie de Bono, they have set up a tech startup that will work directly with landowners. Currently, private landowners tend to sell

their land wholesale for development. Livedin provides the framework for them to implement the infrastructure required for development themselves, realising the retail value for land that is approximately 70 per cent more than they would have got wholesale. The first project, which has received outline planning consent, is a custom-build scheme for 12 houses in the village of Ingoldisthorpe in Norfolk, designed by architects Project Orange with AREA landscape architects. By developing a design code, the custom-build model offers more flexibility and choice to the homebuyer. From a community perspective, there is also the advantage that it encourages landowners with local ties to be responsible for the development phase rather than passing it on to a commercial third party driven solely by profit and remote from neighbours' concerns.

The two partners are also looking to move the practice on by developing an employee ownership scheme. Through a simple trust, Millar + Howard Workshop will be given back to its employees. This is to be advanced in tandem by Millar with the work that he has already undertaken internally on technical reporting documents. By dedicating 10 per cent of their time to sharing knowledge, databases and functions with other small practices, studios, like the workshop, could greatly boost their efficiency and cost base allowing them to optimise on the opportunities that arise out of being small and agile.

Project Orange,
Custom-build housing,
Ingoldisthorpe, Norfolk,
2019

On a greenfield site in the centre of a village, planning consent requires half of the site, including the natural pond, to be retained as publicly accessible land.

DAVID AYRE

Ayre Chamberlain Gaunt

Ayre Chamberlain Gaunt (ACG) was founded in Basingstoke, Hampshire, in 2005 by three directors who met while studying at the University of Portsmouth. As David Ayre describes it, the practice remained 'at the dining table' until 2009 when the three partners took the plunge and gave up their day jobs. Since focusing on the practice full time, Ayre, Matthew Chamberlain and Dominic Gaunt have grown the studio from three to almost 50, garnering awards for their buildings and their practice along the way. They work across a range of sectors, encompassing housing, education, workplace and community. Their most lauded building has been The Point (2016), a youth centre in Tadley, Hampshire. The majority of the practice remains in Basingstoke, with a team of 12 based in an office in London's Oxford Street.

As well as being a project director, overseeing a number of schemes at ACG, Ayre is responsible for practice management, including finance. For him, business acumen is vital in an age when the architectural profession is constantly under pressure, and it is essential that practitioners are able 'to spot opportunity and look to change'. He has started other businesses, such as his own contractor and modular construction company around six years ago. For now, though, the focus is on core business; the sole onus must be on simultaneously 'improving productivity and quality'. Productivity is at the forefront of his mind with the present undercurrent of uncertainty triggered by Brexit. ACG has recently brought in a programming and

David Ayre with members of the team at Ayre Chamberlain Gaunt (ACG), Basingstoke, Hampshire, 2019

A founding director of the practice, David Ayre (on the right) is responsible for its day-to-day management, including finance, in addition to oversight of design projects.

software developer to work alongside the head of technology. This might mean 'one less fee earner' for the practice, but by 'automating repetitive workflow processes' it will 'free up the architects' time'. The next step is to bring in a dedicated project manager. This is how Ayre sees the 'profession changing at pace'. For him, 'this question of what the architecture practice of the future might look like is a constant topic of internal discussion. Could it be more like a design house with programmers, digital artists and project managers working alongside more traditionally trained architects? What is expected from an architect is constantly changing with core skills, making the current educational system irrelevant. It is important to harness individuals into lots of different types of skills. Practice is to have a varied client base beyond those that build buildings. There is a need to be mindful of other industries.'

ACG has already started developing its work beyond the traditional scope of professional services. This includes hosting Common Data Environments for clients, such as local authorities, university estates and developers, to help them manage their built facilities. This leads to a subscription- rather than a fee-based business model and has the advantage of an ongoing income stream. At the other end of the delivery spectrum at RIBA stage 0, like Bryden Wood, Ayre also recognises the new opportunities that are presenting themselves to work with clients and to problem-solve even before a site is found or a brief is introduced. An ongoing relationship with repeat clients is key to this. The architect must have a clear understanding of their business plan and objectives. The practice has, for instance, recently been advising a client on off-site modular construction. It is consultancy work that is in demand and secures a high hourly rate.

To optimise on these new opportunities, Ayre emphasises that 'the profession must move beyond the selling of time – billable hours'. At present, the conventional model of practice rests on 'a fee, risk and time schedule basis'. He sees a new shape of practice emerging: with a stronger offer of upfront client services previous to concept design at stage 1; greater automation of technical design that will make stage 4 less onerous and time consuming; and a new offer of services to clients at stage 7 that will provide a monthly direct-debit income stream based on the performance of buildings. This represents a cultural and mindset shift. Ayre likens it to Apple's business model and the recognition that the money is in software rather than hardware: 'Moving beyond the selling of time, architects should be making money from the running and performance of buildings.'

What is expected from an architect is constantly changing with core skills, making the current educational system irrelevant

Ayre Chamberlain Gaunt (ACG),
The Point,
Tadley, Hampshire,
2016

above and this: A two-storey youth club that was designed in collaboration with its future users, The Point has won both prestigious design and community awards.

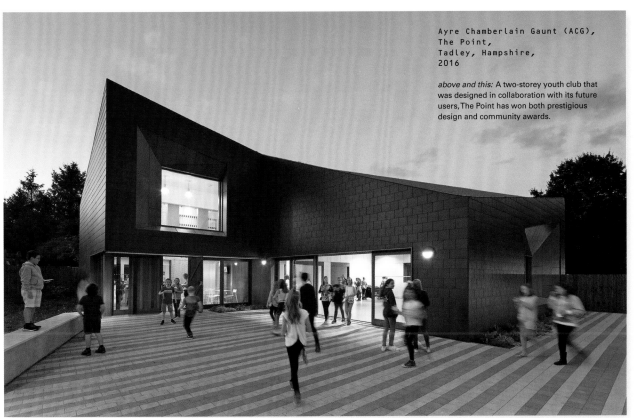

XAVIER DE KESTELIER

HASSELL

The emphasis on new services and technology in architecture must continue to be combined with a design-centric approach if architects are to retain their value and tackle new frontiers. This is highlighted by Xavier De Kestelier, Principal and Head of Design Technology and Innovation at global practice HASSELL. Based in the firm's London office, De Kestelier has an established reputation as a digital pioneer in architecture. Previously a partner and co-head of the Specialist Modelling Group at Foster + Partners, he is also a director of SmartGeometry, a non-profit independent network for computational and digital design specialists that brings together academics and professionals internationally in annual workshops. He warns 'against getting too excited by technology alone – technology has to be an enabler to do greater design'.

Xavier de Kestelier and computational designer Nikos Argyros at Hassell's studio, London, 2019

Though based in London, Xavier De Kestelier (on the right) leads design technology across disciplines and international regions for this global practice.

HASSELL and Eckersley O'Callaghan, Design for human habitation on Mars, NASA 3D Printing Centennial Challenge, 2019

right: Hotel-like in their look and finishes, the living spaces exceed the functional – they are created with the astronauts' comfort in mind.

below: The inflatable habitat protects astronauts from the harsh environment on Mars with a regolith shield.

opposite bottom: The distance of Mars from Earth – 140 million miles (225 million kilometres) – makes a workshop space for fabrication essential for residents: any parts have to be fabricated on Mars rather than sent from Earth.

The emphasis of the project was on human-centric design and developing a place for astronauts to live rather than merely exist as operators

HASSELL has a proven track record in delivering pre-design-stage services to clients. An expert strategy team based in the Melbourne office works globally, consulting with higher education and workplace clients, researching end users' needs and analysing the brief. This is an onus that is led by the firm's Managing Director Steve Cossell, who was previously Australian managing director of international workplace strategy consultancy DEGW. In 2016, HASSELL consolidated this expertise further by merging with FreeState in London, a design group that works with global brands and property developers, creating user-focused stories and immersive experiences. It is a scenario in which, as De Kestelier, explains, 'architecture becomes the hardware for their software'.

In 2019, De Kestelier took HASSELL and architecture into entirely uncharted territory, reaching the final 10 of NASA's 3D Printing Centennial Challenge with its design for an environment for habitation on Mars. The emphasis of the project was on human-centric design and developing a place for astronauts to live rather than merely exist as operators. Aeronautics is a field that until now has been dominated by engineers. This led, in De Kestelier's view, 'to the International Space Station being inefficiently designed. Architects are trained to deal with highly complex systems better than engineers.' Aerospace might be beyond the reach of most practices' aspirations, but this initiative demonstrates the potential for architects to be bold enough to apply their problem-solving and design skills far beyond the scope of traditional services.

Embracing Internal Change

Change is rumbling away on the inside of enlightened practice, and should not be ignored: for the sake of the future of the profession, but also society's far-reaching problems, such as the housing crisis and an outmoded construction industry, which can no longer be solved on the conventional model. In Jamie Johnston's words: 'We can't tinker around the edges by doing what we've always done.' ᗄ

All interviews were undertaken by the author with the featured architects in July 2019.

Notes

1. Ruth Lang, 'Architects Take Command: The LCC Architects' Department', *Volume*, 41 (24), October 2014: http://volumeproject.org/architects-take-command-the-lcc-architects-department/.
2. Claire Jamieson, *The Future for Architects?*, RIBA Building Futures report, 2010, p 25: www.academia.edu/32935719/The_Future_for_Architects. Simon Pepper, Professor of Architecture at the University of Liverpool, is cited as the source of this statistic.
3. From Helen Castle, 'Find Your Inner Entrepreneur', *The RIBA Journal*, 3 January 2017: www.ribaj.com/intelligence/find-your-inner-entrepreneur.
4. *Ibid.*
5. Jaimie Johnston, 'Delivery Platforms for Government Assets: Creating a Marketplace for Manufactured Spaces', Digital Built Britain, July 2017; 'Data Driven Infrastructure: From Digital Tools to Manufactured Components', November 2017; and 'Platforms: Bridging the Gap Between Construction + Manufacturing', March 2018.
6. 'Lean thinking' as propagated by Eric Ries in *The Lean Startup: How Constant Innovation Creates Radically Successful Business*, Portfolio Penguin (London), October 2011.

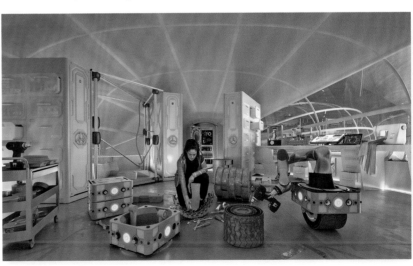

James P Cramer and Scott Simpson

Is Bigger Better?

Wight & Company,
Brother James Gaffney,
FSC Student Center,
Lewis University,
Romeoville, Illinois,
2019

Wight & Company is a design and
delivery firm based in Chicago
and Darien, Illinois. With over 185
professionals and a multidisciplinary
expertise in commercial, corporate,
education, government and public
use markets, the firm heralds its
75th year with illustrious integrated
AEC excellence.

The Rise of Specialisation in Professional Practice

Does the risk-averse environment of the construction industry bring with it possible advantages of specialisation? **James P Cramer and Scott Simpson**, respectively a founder and senior fellow of the Design Futures Council international organisation, guide us through specific examples where firms have prospered through concentration on the delivery of certain types of buildings and have expanded the expertise of their staff outside the traditional architectural sphere to provide their clients with a more seamless service.

Here is a situation we have all encountered: you meet someone new, and the initial banter covers the basics: Where are you from? What do you do? And so forth. If the person happens to be a doctor or a lawyer, the next question is automatic: What *kind* of physician (or attorney) are you? We take it for granted that most medical and legal professionals are specialists of some kind. You would not visit a podiatrist if you had a vision problem, nor would you entrust your estate planning to a criminal defence lawyer.

This same phenomenon is fast taking hold in the world of architecture, engineering and construction (AEC) services. As projects become larger and more complex, they require an increasing number of specialists to handle both the big picture and the details. Clients are changing, too; it is now fairly common to engage professional programme managers to oversee the project team, which in turn affects the decision-making process. The result is a very different dynamic in how buildings get designed, documented and delivered, and it has long-term implications for the design professions.

It was not that long ago that many, if not most, design firms could lay claim to being generalist in nature, preferring not to be pigeonholed into doing just one type of building. After all, the essence of design thinking is to synthesise information and ideas from a variety of sources and apply them creatively to solve just about any problem. Architects therefore preferred to be ecumenical in their approach, if only to avoid the temptation of formulaic thinking. When specialised skills or knowledge were required, consultants could easily be engaged to fill the gaps. As a result, a substratum of specialised consultants began to develop, covering such areas as programming, specifications, lighting, acoustics, geotechnical engineering, food service, security, vertical transportation, curtain walling, parking, building codes, and so forth. Of course, this was in addition to the usual structural, mechanical, electrical and plumbing engineering required on most jobs. Thus, designing a building became somewhat like making a movie: you needed to line up the screenwriter, director, actors, cinematographer, costume designer, sound engineer and a host of others to produce the film. (Just watch the credits roll at the end of any movie to see how many different skills are required.) When the work was done, the crew disbanded (though they might reassemble in different combinations for subsequent projects). Architectural teams operated on the same basic principles.

Clients became more specialised as well, especially as owners began to see design as a value-added service, integral to their business strategy. They were increasingly focused on return on investment (ROI) rather than initial capital cost, and they wanted to make sure that they chose a project team that had particular expertise in the given project type. This was particularly true for projects such as healthcare, higher education, hospitality and institutional work. Clients realised that they required more skills to deal with the complexities involved, which included not only the usual aesthetics and engineering issues, but also the zoning regulations, building codes, financing, public approvals process, marketing and leasing, not to mention the actual operations and management of the building (now called an 'asset') when it was finally put into service. Sophisticated clients became aware that the capital cost of a new project was in fact a small fraction of the long-term cost of ownership, and this affected how teams were assembled and decisions got made.

New Competitive Shifts and Vertical Integration
While all this was going on, other important changes were taking place in the marketplace, not the least of which was an increased awareness of the importance of sustainable design and the introduction of sophisticated technologies such as building information modelling (BIM) and 3D printers, as well as new delivery paradigms such as design/build and integrated project delivery (IPD). So, the AEC industry evolved quickly and in fundamental ways. This was reflected in the size and complexity of projects, business objectives of the owners, composition and management of the professional teams, nature of design deliverables, and even construction technology (drones, robotics, prefabrication). It quickly became a whole new ball game.

Savvy offices of all sizes have adapted to this new landscape. Over the past decade, the profession has seen a wave of mergers and acquisitions that formalised what used to be ad-hoc networks of firms working together. There is now a plethora of high-profile practices (such as Jacobs, Stantec and AECOM), operating both nationally and internationally, which are able to offer vertically integrated services rather than relying on horizontal networks of consultants. These large firms employ hundreds (and in many cases, thousands) of staff and are operated as true businesses, with management focusing on key performance indicators as well as creative design solutions.

This new way of doing business has some distinct advantages. For example, consider the market for healthcare facilities. A multi-trillion-dollar enterprise, the healthcare industry has become highly regulated – and highly politicised. Funding approvals for new construction can be complex,

as can reimbursement policies, which are often set by third parties, such as the Federal government in the case of Medicare, and insurance companies in the case of employer-provided health plans. These factors weigh very heavily on the physical design and the day-to-day management of healthcare facilities. The economics are such that the independent local community hospital, which used to be the primary venue for delivering most patient services, is no longer viable. Instead, medical networks have been forged that offer integrated services in a variety of settings, including local clinics, surgicentres, emergency medicine and tertiary care facilities. A typical client may own and operate dozens (or even hundreds) of locations within the network, offering a wide range of specialities. The economy of scale is obvious, and it is easy to see that such enterprises require a far different approach to design and construction.

Specialisation in Large Firm Practice
In response, some design offices have chosen to specialise in one or more specific project types, and there are even specialities within specialities, such as those that do walk-in clinics or surgicentres rather than inpatient facilities. Like their clients, these practices have become vertically integrated, offering all the required services in-house. Many operate as architectural/engineering firms and include standard structural, mechanical, electrical and plumbing engineering as well. This not only helps with coordination during the design and documentation phases, but also enables them to retain substantial fees and thus increase profits while at the same time lowering liability. In a healthcare facility, mechanical, electrical and plumbing (MEP) systems can easily represent 40 per cent of the capital cost of construction and more than 60 per cent of the operational cost, so offering integrated services from a single source makes a great deal of sense for both the design professional and the client.

HDR,
Parkland Hospital,
Dallas, Texas,
2019

HDR employs more than 10,000 people worldwide and serves 14 markets including healthcare, where it sub-specialises in acute care, ambulatory care, behavioural health and translational health. While its multidisciplinary AEC expertise is high profile, its success is underscored by a unifying commitment to the community – to over 100 years in the making.

Some healthcare firms have taken specialisation and vertical integration a step further, adding medical and nursing specialists or even hospital administrators to their staff. Others offer medical equipment planning (and in some cases even procurement and installation). This enables them to truly speak the client's language and provide a perspective that a conventional architectural or architectural/engineering practice cannot.

This trend towards vertical integration can also be seen in other markets, including office buildings, hospitality, retail, higher education and large-scale residential projects. Such firms have greater critical mass, experience and marketing clout, and a broader geographic reach; and they offer staff a wider range of career paths (which often come with the higher salaries that are justified by specialised skills). It should come as no surprise that clients seek out specialist firms when contemplating significant projects, and in many cases the mega-firms are able to offer competitive fees even for very small jobs. The biggest clients will sometimes engage a single firm to provide comprehensive services for all their projects nationally and internationally, thus creating a strategic partnership. Formidable competition, indeed.

Some firms are now also addressing the traditional divide between design and delivery by offering integrated design/build services. They not only have architects and engineers on staff; they can construct what they design. The potential advantages of this approach are huge, as it streamlines the inherent inefficiencies that are baked into the conventional design/bid/build process, in which 30 per cent of projects fail to meet schedule or budget. The economics are compelling: higher fees, lower risk, better cost control and document coordination, and greater profits. An integrated design/delivery approach can also greatly enhance quality control on site and reduce liability claims since everyone is playing for the same team, working in concert rather than at cross purposes. This strategy works only if the organisation is vertically integrated, and it is increasingly being adopted by major construction-management companies, which are adding design capability to their range of services. It is easy to see that the implications for architecture-only or even architecture/engineering firms are significant.

Small-Firm Impact
Scale is important. If a firm is big enough, it can afford to specialise; and if it can specialise sufficiently, it can provide the vertically integrated services that few competitors offer, thus creating a unique market advantage. Where does this leave the small practice? This is not to say that small firms cannot compete effectively. There will always be a place for boutique designers who choose to develop expertise in a single market, project type or service specialisation.

As part of an ongoing research project on small-firm success in collaboration supported by the American Institute of Architects (AIA) and Design Futures Council, the US architecture market was canvassed for exemplars of firms that model specialisation and also produce compelling design. The list of nominations numbered more than 65 small practices – each smaller than 10 total staff, including owners – among them 4RM+ULA (St Paul, Minnesota), HL Design Build (Phoenix, Arizona), Salmela Architect (Duluth, Minnesota),

HL Design Build,
Sanctuary Camelback Mountain Resort and Spa,
Paradise Valley, Arizona,
2018

This small design/build enterprise has a large-scale impact. With international work spanning hospitality, residential and commercial sectors, it has transformed the design and construction industry through the unifying desire it shares with its clients: 'to live elegantly and uniquely'.

4RM+ULA,
Target Field Station,
Minneapolis, Minnesota,
2018

A phonetic acronym for Form + Urban Landscape Articulation, 4RM+ULA has built a niche in urban redevelopment. Its award-winning designs infuse function and innovation with art and tradition, respectively, to provide high-quality architecture to areas traditionally underserved by the profession.

Firm	Location	Specialty	Size (FTE)
BLDGS	Atlanta, GA	Higher Education & Public Use	5
Becker + Becker	New Haven, CT	Developer Architect	4
4RM+ULA	St. Paul, MN	Urban Redevelopment	7
HL Design Build, LLC	Phoenix, AZ	Hospitality & Design/Build Residential	6
Hollander Design Group	San Diego, CA	Corporate Offices & the Arts	8
Marlon Blackwell	Fayetteville, AK	Design-Intensive Generalist	1
Rick Ryniak Architects	Maui, Hawaii	Custom Residential	1
Salmela Architects	Duluth, MN	Scandinavian Modern/Mixed Use	3.5
Shepherd Resources, Inc./AIA	Beaver Creek, CO	Custom Residential & Resort	7
Vera Iconica Architecture	Jackson Hole, WY	Wellness Architecture & Residential	5
Williston Enterprises	Greenville, NC	"Experience" Design & Charettes	1

James P Cramer and Scott Simpson,
Small-Firm Success,
2019

With the backing of the American Institute of
Architects (AIA) and Design Futures Council, the
authors undertook a two-year study of small-firm
success in the US. After reviewing more than
65 small practices, they chose 11 exemplars for
further analysis – all with a staff under 10.

Shepherd Resources (Beaver Creek, Colorado) and Vera
Iconica Architecture (Jackson, Wyoming).

These firms have been able to differentiate themselves
even in a highly competitive market, and even the smallest
among them are thriving in an age of specialisation and
acceleration. Data was collected in 45 categories. Key
findings were that the average number of employees was
5.05; the average annual revenue per firm was $1,255,229, or
$243,734 per FTE; and on a scale of 5, the level of professional
satisfaction among the firm leaders was rated 4.91.

Offices like these are unlikely to attract the largest-scale
commissions, and even if they did it is unlikely they would
be designated the lead firm of record. Clearly size matters.
And yet, as these firms prove, the smallest of offices can have
exemplary experiences both in business terms and as high-
profile designers.

The phenomenon of specialisation is not new. There
are countless examples of industries that, when in their
nascent stages, spawned numerous competing startups
that eventually congealed to become larger, more dominant

Shepherd Resources,
Inc/AIA, Watersong,
Steamboat Springs, Colorado,
2019

With a staff of seven, the office is known for creating
fine homes on remarkable properties – primarily in
its Vail/Beaver Creek backyard playground. To say
its client list is enviable is an understatement. Its
unofficial motto? 'Any perfect job is acceptable.'

Vera Iconica Architecture,
Walker Residence,
Wilson, Wyoming,
2019

Founded in 2010 by then 27-year-old Veronica
Schreibeis Smith, the practice has built a design
reputation at the forefront of wellness trends.
Most recently it launched the Vera Iconica
Wellness Kitchen design range.

Salmela Architect,
Family Retreat,
Duluth, Minnesota,
2018

David Salmela is known for his enviable,
decorated brand of Scandinavian modern.
He believes most architects do their best
work in places of familiarity and thus
adopts a regional approach that combines
a deep appreciation for climate and place
with an ongoing investment in long-term
relationships.

In the years to come we may well see sub-specialities of design becoming more formally recognised, and even a certification process that subdivides the profession into smaller fiefdoms

players. Examples include banks, software developers, car manufacturers and media companies. The advantages of scale are undeniable, but it is important not to lose the core competency that makes design firms valuable in the first place: the ability to produce creative solutions.

Indeed, it seems that success can inevitably lead to scale. There are many good examples of smaller practices that have morphed into mid-size or even much larger firms over time. It is instructive to note that the largest design firm in the US, Gensler, started out as a three-person office. Cambridge Seven – now a 50-staff firm – became well known working with Buckminster Fuller on a single building: the US pavilion at the Montreal Expo in 1964 (the same exposition that showcased a then-young and unknown Moshe Safdie's famous Habitat housing development). C-7, as it has become known, is now one of the leading mid-size firms in the country. Wight & Co of Chicago is a third-generation family-owned firm of 185 staff that has grown significantly in size and impact by adopting an integrated design/build strategy. Payette Associates of Boston (staff 175) began as a boutique firm specialising in medical planning and is now widely recognised as a leader not just in healthcare, but also in research facilities for colleges and universities worldwide. By choice, it has always practised in a single location and has resisted growth by merger and acquisition.

The Future of Specialisation

As technology continues to advance, more and more of the creative aspects of design will be automated. For example, in a standard AIA contract, construction documents account for 40 per cent of the base fee. Technology has already automated significant aspects of structural and mechanical design, and this can easily be extended to include stairs, elevators, building envelopes, roofing, glazing and so on. One possible impact of increased automation would be to shift more fees to the creative phases of the project (schematic design and design development), but another could be to make design fees vulnerable to commoditisation – just as has happened in the banking and investment industries.

In the years to come we may well see sub-specialities of design becoming more formally recognised, and even a certification process that subdivides the profession into smaller fiefdoms, just like medicine. (Radiologists are not licensed to do surgery, and cardiologists do not deliver babies.) Sub-specialities such as paediatric anaesthesiology are now board certified. Could this same trend hold true for architects? This has important implications for the entire design and construction industry, and especially how architects are trained, licensed and compensated. Thus, in the future, it could well be that when you meet new people and discover that they are architects, your second question will automatically be: 'What kind of architects are you?' ∅

Text © 2020 John Wiley & Sons Ltd. Images: pp 50–51 Courtesy of Wight & Company. Photography by Paul Schlismann Photography; p 53 Courtesy of HDR. Photography by Farshid Assassi; p 54(t) Courtesy of HL Design Build, LLC. Photography by Michael Baxter; p 54(b) Courtesy of 4RM+ULA. Photography by Farm Kid Studios, Inc; p 55(t) Courtesy of Austin Cramer; p 55(b) Courtesy of Shepherd Resources, Inc / AIA. Photography by Andrew Wellman; pp 56-7(t) Courtesy of Salmela Architect. Photography by Paul Crosby; p 56(b) Courtesy of Vera Iconica Architecture. Photography by David Agnello

Design, Data and Liveability

Ben van Berkel

The Role of Technology Within the Future of an Expanded Profession

UNStudio and UNSense,
Brainport Smart District,
Helmond, The Netherlands,
2018–

Data and services platform. The district's technology universe is introduced as a framework for sharing data and information in order to enrich the efficiency of the landscapes, buildings and public spaces, while offering seamless connectivity.

Ben van Berkel, co-founder of Amsterdam-based UNStudio, believes that architectural practice has been invigorated by the myriad of cultural, societal and technologic parameters that a contemporary architect must consider. The practice recently formed a spinoff company, UNSense, to develop and commercialise technologies emerging out of UNStudio's smart city and smart environment projects. Here he describes some of the products, prototypes and startups the studio has developed to help tackle some of the important issues of our time: stress, urban water and climate change.

The architectural profession has always experienced change and architects have continuously been required to expand their roles and techniques. In fact, their specialised capabilities have emerged from the effects of these developments. Le Corbusier and Frank Lloyd Wright developed special drawing techniques to accomplish their work, even though they were working with small teams. We are fortunate that change has happened in our time as professionals also. The world and the profession are now driven by digital technology, but also by many other technological, societal, environmental and cultural forces.
As a result, the role of the architect is enriched and is expanding today. However, this expansion of practice requires an entrepreneurial spirit from architects and firm leaders.

This expansion can be thought about in terms of both architectural *hardware* and *software*. The hardware aspects of the profession are those related to technology and to new efficiency models. For example, UNStudio has a specialist building information modelling (BIM) team, like many firms. But now sensor technology has arrived, providing visibility into the performance of the building. As a result, we also need specialists in both building systems and sensor technologies within the profession.

The software, or softer side of the profession, consists of the cultural qualities that architects can, and should, bring to the project. This cultural side is also experiencing expansion. It may seem paradoxical to say that the cultural qualities of the profession expand through technology, but that is the case. Le Corbusier was influenced by the visual arts, while Bernard Tschumi has been inspired by cinematographers like Eisenstein. Now it is possible for architects to be influenced by any number of cultural references, whilst simultaneously addressing concerns such as health, sustainability and circularity of services. Architects are now in a position to connect themselves to all of these fields holistically, thereby bringing more to their practice and to the profession.

Technology contributes significantly to the possible expansion of both architectural hardware and software, as it can have extremely positive effects in terms of the ways it guides how we live, how we work and how we learn. Today architects can design with data. However, to do so successfully, technology needs to be guided: data requires direction in order to give it form and colour. New sensor technologies can bring architects closer to the users of their buildings. The data collected by sensor systems ostensibly enables architects to design with the end user: discovering what they need, what they enjoy and what kind of flexibility they require in a building.

In 2018 UNStudio founded a sister company, UNSense, the main aim of which is to use technology to create better human-centric spaces. UNSense, unlike the more common smart city concepts, goes beyond mere efficiency and performance-related goals, instead designing for positive human, societal and environmental impact. It is the belief at UNSense that such considerations should always guide the development, innovation and implementation of technological solutions. This is also essential to avoid 'tech push' by technology solution providers.

Entrepreneurialism:
Organisation and Leadership
UNStudio's response to recent expansions within the profession has required a great deal of new thinking about how the practice is organised and managed. As a result, the firm invests in knowledge and business management platforms. There are a number of different, specialised platforms within the organisation: a sustainability platform, a BIM platform, a new materials platform, and better archiving systems.

The most recent addition is a dedicated futures team, and one of their most successful products is consultancy. As a result, the Futures Group at UNStudio is now operating at a profit, just as the design units do. Many clients are now concerned with the kinds of buildings they will need in the future. Prior to the financial crisis of 2008, there was a significant focus on the building as icon, functioning as it did as an element of the client's branding. However, since then the focus has shifted towards building performance. Today buildings need to be healthy, attractive, comfortable and productive to work in. However, these priorities are constantly changing. As such, UNStudio's Futures Group works with clients to forecast potential developments in the future requirements of buildings and cities. These types of projects would have been unexpected a year ago, but the Futures Group has been the firm's best recent investment, alongside UNSense.

However, there needs to be a reciprocity between design and technology, between the hardware and

UNStudio and UNSense,
Diagram of the innovation ecosystem,
2018

The sister companies partner on many projects but
have different areas of focus, different expertise and
are structured separately to support the necessary
dynamics of the architecture and tech business models.

Living | Work | Mobility

UNS
UNSTUDIO

Design | Knowledge Future → UNSENSE

Hardware | Software

software. Today architecture has to be technologically
driven to a certain extent, but the role of the architect
needs to become more holistic. The architect needs to
be a *cultural entrepreneur*: interested in business, but
also with a genuine fascination for culture. This cultural
side needs to be cultivated even more than it has been
by the discipline to date, so that architecture does not
provide merely a one-dimensional reading. Choices
need to be made about what the practice will address,
whilst simultaneously maintaining a holistic approach.
This entails learning to understand how to be a better
leader in order to guide the different facets and the
people within the company – from interior design to
technical people and data specialists. It is especially
important to support people who are good at the craft
of the profession, because while the craft is vital, it is
not in fact well protected by the profession.

Unlike UNStudio's Knowledge and Futures platforms
however, UNSense was set up as its own entity – a
company of companies separate from UNStudio.
A year was spent trying to see if UNSense could be
incorporated as a unit within the architectural studio.
In the end, however, it became clear that it needed to
be organised differently, because little of the tech world
fits within the business model of an architectural office.
UNSense consults and creates design interventions
and products. It works with specialist designers and
technical experts: data scientists, sensor engineers, and
programmers. To support the products in particular,
significant investment is required in the beginning
and these entities each need their own organisations:
small subsidiary companies have to be set up for each
product, in order to create opportunities for both people
and investors, and to find bespoke and innovative ways
to go to market. The Managing Director of UNSense
comes from the financial world and originally wanted

to be an architect, but went to business school instead.
While architects are interested in becoming managers
of these companies, they do not yet have the training
and experience. It can take a long time to get the right
people in the right places, and a certain degree of luck
is required to find the people with the right skills and
knowledge. The ambition is that in five to 10 years'
time, UNSense and UNStudio will be able to join
together again, but at this point they can only operate
separately. There is however a great deal they can learn
from each other in the meantime.

In terms of what is required of firm leaders,
ultimately they need to be a combination of Steve
Jobs and Richard Branson. Like Jobs, they need to
follow their goals and ambitions, to be clear and
very visionary. At the same time, they must avoid
pure autocracy and operate collaboratively and
democratically, like Branson. Such an approach is
necessary in order to nurture, keep and optimise the
talent they have in-house. It is often said that the
profession is slow. This is because it can easily take six
or seven years of continuous work before a large-scale
building is actually built. That is why the team needs
to stay together. It is not productive to have a lot of
changes within the team, and this means that the firm's
leader needs to be very altruistic to succeed.

Integrating Technology:
Living Laboratories
The Paris Agreement in Europe now means that all
countries need to achieve set CO_2 reduction targets,
and the Netherlands is determined to meet these goals.
Dutch policies mean that the Netherlands will be ready
to transform its existing houses and buildings to be
energy neutral. The aim is also to replace the use of
natural gas in all homes with electricity, and there is

currently a great deal of discussion about mobility as well – for instance using more electric bikes and reducing the number of cars. But there is also a great deal of research and experimentation taking place in the Netherlands with respect to densification, and how to establish new neighbourhoods that can incorporate emerging technologies to sustain growing populations.

A good example of this is the Brainport Smart District (2018–), a project in Helmond, near Eindhoven, where a large number of big technology companies are located. UNStudio has designed the urban vision for this new neighbourhood, while UNSense plays a key role in the planned use of technology. The district will support a combination of living and working. Ninety per cent of services will be circular, including 100 per cent energy neutrality and self-supporting water systems. Food production aims to create new forms of community building. People will be able to enjoy shared gardens, where they can produce food for themselves and the community, should they wish. Forty per cent of the required food can be produced in the district, and 60 per cent within a radius of 100 kilometres (62 miles).

Underlying the project will be a data platform, which will make it possible to monitor the performance of the different building systems for all of the 1,500 houses. The data platform is set up as a separate company in order to be able to involve other small investors.

UNSense is starting with an experiment involving 100 houses. The project is intended to research and develop new models in which inhabitants of the district as a whole can benefit directly from data. UNSense wants to investigate what happens when data is used for the benefit of the community. For instance, residents in the neighbourhood could organise themselves in order to exert more influence on, for example, how mobility and energy are organised. However the residents remain the owners of their own data at all times. They decide whether or not they want to take part in an experiment. To guarantee this, a trusted body is currently being formulated that can provide a guarantee for experiments, so that residents can see whether they meet requirements on privacy, property, security and ethical considerations.

UNStudio and UNSense,
Brainport Smart District,
Helmond, The Netherlands,
2018–

right: Catering to new local and international users, Brainport Smart District is seeking early adopters of new ways of living and working.

below: Circular services strategies for electricity, water and food. This district of 1,500 houses will be able to generate almost all of its own services.

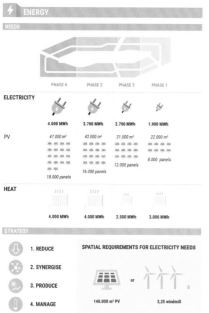

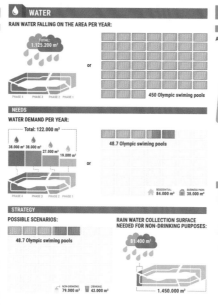

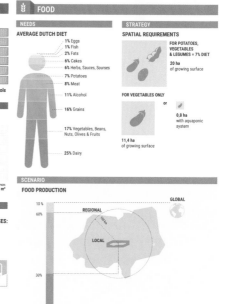

Developing New Technologies on the Product Scale

In addition to urban projects, UNStudio and UNSense are involved in the research and development of new architectural products, one of which is a new photovoltaic (PV) module which can be used as cladding for the building envelope. High-rise buildings do not have enough roof surface to accommodate the amount of solar panels that would be needed to make the buildings net zero, and whilst building-integrated photovoltaics (BIPV) have made steps in the right direction, they do not offer a complete design solution for architects. This is why UNStudio's Knowledge team originally worked on the research, design and development of a new technology for aesthetic solar-panel cladding modules for full facade integration. This research and development was carried out as part of a European research project and in collaboration with the Construct PV consortium. The product is called Solar Visuals and is now approved and can be implemented. However, as it needs to go to market in innovative ways, UNSense joined forces with the printing company TS Visuals and 'ECN part of TNO' (the Energy Research Centre within The Netherlands Organisation for applied scientific research). Currently companies are being selected to partner with and to invest in this product, including large glass companies, while the modules undergo further development.

Another product that UNSense is developing is RESET (2017), which was first prototyped by UNStudio and SCAPE at the Salone del Mobile in Milan. There, RESET was organised as a series of pods that featured scientifically proven stress-reduction methods in a playful and interactive way. It was designed to empower people to deal with stress more effectively. Everything visitors did in the pods was measured by sensors. These sensors traced the visitor's response to the stress-reduction experiences and provided real-time 'factual' feedback. UNSense is now talking to travel tech companies, investigating possibilities to install similar RESET pods in high-stress spaces, such as airports or work settings.

UNStudio and UNSense,
Solar Visuals printed solar panels,
Amsterdam, The Netherlands,
2018

Solar Visuals, founded by UNSense and partners ECN part of TNO and printing specialist TS Visuals, is a startup named after a new, revolutionary, energy-producing cladding material that can be integrated in facades of buildings.

UNStudio and SCAPE,
Prototype RESET stress-reduction pods,
Salone del Mobile,
Milan, Italy,
2017

RESET is a technology product – a sensored space designed to help users reduce their stress levels through biofeedback, which is currently being further developed by UNSense.

Futurism and the Future
of Architecture

As previously mentioned, the profession is slow. This means that architects always have to look towards the future: what kind of society will we be living in in 10 years' time? Will all vehicles be electric? Will roads be automatically responsive to traffic flows? What will this mean for the infrastructure in and around our cities? Perhaps the resulting noise and fume reduction will mean that previously unused land close to ring roads can be developed, making these valuable areas of the city habitable. In light of this, in 2016, UNStudio carried out an urban study investigating how the A10 ring road around Amsterdam could possibly be developed in the future. UNStudio carried out another urban vision in 2018, for the Central Innovation District (CID) test site in The Hague. This 'Socio-Technical City of the Future' investigates how an area like the CID, despite extremely high density in the future, can become self-sufficient and energy-neutral.

UNStudio,
Urban study of the A10 ring road and Lelylaan area,
Amsterdam, The Netherlands,
2016

Commissioned by the Royal Institute of Dutch Architects (BNA), in consultation with the Rijkswaterstaat (Ministry of Infrastructure and Water Management) and Amsterdam City Council, UNStudio collaborated on a study that examines the future potential for the integration of infrastructure and city development around Amsterdam's A10 ring road.

UNStudio,
Socio-Technical City of the Future,
The Hague, The Netherlands,
2018

In UNStudio's future vision, the Central Innovation District (CID) becomes a green, self-sufficient double-layered zone, where a new urban layer of housing, offices, urban mobility and park-like public space is created over the existing train-track infrastructure.

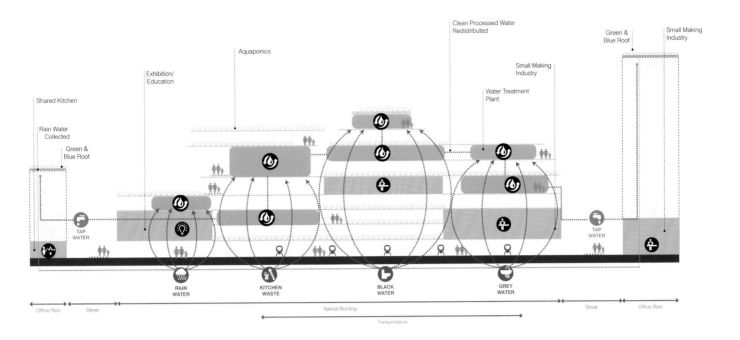

above: Section of the Biopolus, which is one of the 'gateway' structures within the Socio-Technical City and comprises an urban irrigation system with wadis, water squares, canals and waterfalls.

UNSense is also currently working with a number of cities with respect to the future use of smart technologies. These enquiries are coming from cities like Amsterdam and The Hague, but also from cities in Asia. Many cities have spoken to the bigger tech companies about this ambition but have not been satisfied with what these companies can provide. As a result, they are now asking UNStudio and UNSense to help them with a new kind of design problem: how can they use smart technologies in order to improve their communities?

Back in the early 1980s, there was great excitement in the field, especially at the Architectural Association (AA) in London, where the group of so-called 'paper architects' – which included Zaha Hadid at the time – was producing big drawings and axonometrics. If this current phase is done well, the next 10 to 20 years could be even more exciting than that period was. In the not too distant future, architecture firms will become tech companies. They will employ programmers and tech specialists, as well as designers. There will also be many more and varied specialists within the broader practice. These specialists will not only focus on the building scale, but also on the product and urban scales. The hope is that the education of design will also focus much more on technology. Today it is very hard to find good designers who have enough knowledge about technology to be able to truly understand how to integrate it into design and how to design with data. But this is what the future holds and, as such, perhaps now more than ever before, firm leaders have to put their entrepreneurial skills into action in order to remain relevant within this new, expanded profession. ⌂

Brad Samuels

MIN THE

ARCHITECTURE AND THE ABSURDITY OF SELF-IMPOSED LIMITATION

SITU Research, Akshay Mehra and Adam Maloof,
Grinding imaging and reconstruction instrument (GIRI),
Department of Geoscience,
Princeton University, New Jersey,
2013

GIRI was designed in collaboration with Princeton geoscientist Professor
Adam Maloof. Developed to assist in the study of early animal life, it was
used for analysis and identification of the Trezona fossil specimen, now
established as the oldest animal ever discovered.

Based in New York, **Brad Samuels** is a founding partner and
Director of Research at SITU, an unorthodox architectural practice
that is embracing the massive change that technology and
work patterns are forcing on the making of architecture. SITU's
multidisciplinary staff actively try to engage with and provide
insight into 'the problem of living'.

Managing the interface between
physical and digital workflows is
central to SITU's business model.

```
1   import proj4 from 'proj4'
2   import {PLYLoader} from 'three/examples/jsm/loaders/PLYLoader'
3   import * as d3 from 'd3'
4
5   proj4.defs([
6     [
7       'EPSG:32718',
8       '+proj=utm +zone=18 +south +ellps=WGS84 +datum=WGS84 +units=m +no_defs '],
9     [
10      'EPSG:4326',
11      '+proj=longlat +ellps=WGS84 +datum=WGS84 +no_defs']
12  ]);
13
14  self.onmessage = ({data}) => {
15    // const (name, attributes) = object;
16    var loader = new PLYLoader();
17    loader.load(data.path, (object) => {
18      const attributes = object.attributes
19      let pointData = []
20      let positions = attributes.position.array;
21      let colors = attributes.color.array
22
23      let thresh = 1-data.dec_level
24
25      for (let i = 0;  i < attributes.position.array.length; i+=3){
26        if (Math.random() > thresh){
27          continue
28        }
29        else{
30          let coords = [positions[i], positions[i+1]]
31          coords.push(positions[i+2] - 4320)
32          pointData.push({
33            position: [coords[0],coords[1],coords[2]], |
34            normal: [0,0,1],
35            color: [Math.floor(colors[i]*255), Math.floor(colors[i+1]*255), Math.floor(colors[i+2]*255), 230]
36          })
37        }
38      }
39      self.postMessage({pd: pointData, positions: positions, colors: colors, count: attributes.position.count});
40
41    });
42  };
```

Accelerated, massive change is sweeping across our disciplines, services and modes of production. Media, logistics, defence, retail, finance – nothing is immune. We are experiencing shifts not only in models of practice, but also in the evolving standard for what we can expect the rate of change to be. As part of this process, existing corporate structures are being radically refigured to embrace different forms of management and hierarchy.

What opportunities and threats do these shifts bring to architecture? While it is exciting to be living and working through this period of rapid transformation, it is worth noting that the field is poised precariously between the glacial pace of regulatory transformation that defines certain aspects of professional practice, and the rate at which the technology and tools of the discipline continue to change. We may be reaching a tipping point as we approach the convergence of the Internet of Things (IOT) and the Cloud – a moment at which the built environment and the data landscape will begin to deliver on the promise of a seamless physical/digital experience. If so, this is a critical moment for architects to stake a claim on the future of practice and, perhaps most importantly, a moment to either assert relevance or cede agency.

To assert relevance, we should first recognise that architecture currently sits adrift between professional orthodoxies codified generations ago and the tightening grip of evangelical technocrats who are actively stalking market share of all that touches the built environment. As we think about the changing definitions of architecture, it will help to consider how shifting forms of practice will refigure the role of the architect as they simultaneously also deplete the talent pool. How does the field remain relevant as big tech lures young designers away by providing a better culture, better pay and the promise of greater impact?

One Model

Amid a sea change in the discipline, many new models of practice are emerging. An unconventional architecture practice that uses design, research and fabrication for social and creative impact, SITU has been shaped by a conviction that creative work should not be limited by the specialisation of disciplines. For this reason, its staff includes architects, computer scientists, lawyers, geographers, artists, anthropologists, furniture makers, planners, engineers, filmmakers and many more. This diversity of backgrounds enriches the firm's approach to architecture, but more importantly it has allowed SITU to become involved in work both within and well beyond the traditional boundaries of the discipline. From ongoing work with the International Criminal Court to introduce new forms of spatial analysis for forums of justice, to working with geologists at Princeton University to analyse and identify the earliest forms of animal life, it has become clear that architects' education, tools and processes bring great value to other fields.

In addition to the practice's interdisciplinary DNA, its physical infrastructure also plays an important role. Split between creative studio and industrial workshop, SITU's

SITU Research,
International Criminal Court evidentiary platform,
Timbuktu,
Mali,
2016

Digital evidentiary platform designed and built for the International
Criminal Court's trial of Ahmad Al Faqi Al Mahdi, who was charged
with the destruction of sites of cultural heritage in Timbuktu in 2012
and 2013. He pleaded guilty and was sentenced to nine years in prison.

James Turrell,
Three Saros,
New York,
2015

SITU Fabrication served as the specialty consultant for the engineering and
fabrication of this art installation within a midtown Manhattan office building.
The project required an efficient approach to construction and coordination
among various design teams given the complexity of its geometry and site-
specific nature of the work.

SITU's setup enables
a unique sort of
radical pragmatism –
experimenting with new
material possibilities
as they are imagined

setup enables a unique sort of radical pragmatism –
experimenting with new material possibilities as they
are imagined – whether that means realising technically
challenging installations with artists such as James
Turrell, or prototyping and fabricating the firm's own
projects to address gaps the market is yet to identify
or fill.

Through the diversity of staff backgrounds, the range
of projects and the co-location of tools for both thinking
and making, SITU has positioned itself to engage fluidly
across a range of creative work. Though this is just one
model, it is emblematic of an approach that needs to be
reconciled with both traditional forms of practice and a
rapidly evolving field.

Shifting Definitions
The future of the discipline is often discussed in legal,
technological or market terms – conversations that elide
the foundational question: what do we mean when
we use the word 'architecture'? Part of the challenge
of answering this question is the often-limited way
we think about the idea of the profession itself. For
example, how can the quickly evolving aspects of
contemporary practice be reconciled with the conceits
of organisations such as the American Institute of
Architects (AIA) that have doubled down on the
relevance of professionalisation with all of its vestiges?

This is not a new question. Consider others who
have sought to reset the agenda. Bernard Rudofsky's
prescient introduction in the catalogue for the 1964
'Architecture Without Architects' exhibition at the
Museum of Modern Art (MoMA) in New York remains
relevant today:

> Part of our troubles results from the tendency to
> ascribe to architects – or, for that matter, to all
> specialists – exceptional insight into problems of
> living when, in truth, most of them are concerned
> with problems of business and prestige. Besides
> the art of living is neither taught nor encouraged
> in this country.[1]

In contemporary terms, it is this 'insight into the
problems of living' that remains acutely important
and largely missing in the business (market) and
prestige (professionalisation) of architecture today.
If we interpret Rudofsky's prompt as a challenge to
remain focused on the definition of architecture while
expanding the idea of who can/should function as an
architect, the current relevance of the MoMA exhibition
becomes a structural inversion – the 'vernacular,
anonymous, spontaneous, indigenous, rural'[2] examples
of 1964 have been replaced by the indispensable work
of other outsiders: computer scientists, geographers,
biologists, construction managers and so on. While
the invocation of 'non-pedigreed' actors in this context
is describing groups other than those featured in the
exhibition, the absurdity of self-imposed limitation that
Rudofsky aptly identifies remains absolutely the same
core issue.

Structural Obstacles

This essay is neither a flight of philosophy nor a wholesale indictment of professional practice. Nor does it attempt to litigate the existence of licensure in architecture. Rather, it calls our attention to the implications and consequences of the yawning disconnect between change and regulations that illuminate how the design professional is increasingly out of touch. Looking at architecture in the context of the radical shifts across other industries, we can identify and isolate the statutes and regulations that alienate the 'capital A' Architect from contemporary practice. And while we parse the relevant rules of licensure and registration from the vestigial ones, we should also interrogate why such regulation exists in the first place. A body of historical and sociological scholarship, too rich to be examined in detail here, chronicles the rise of professional practice across disciplines at the turn of the 20th century.

Consider first how the New York State guidelines that govern professional practice, when broadly interpreted, prevent an architecture firm from effectively engaging in interdisciplinary work. Article 21.1b4 of the Rules of the Board of Regents for New York State stipulates that 'Unprofessional conduct in the practice of any profession licensed, certified or registered pursuant to title VIII … shall include: permitting any person to share in the fees for professional services, other than: a partner, employee, associate in a professional firm or corporation, professional subcontractor or consultant authorized to practice the same profession.'[3] At least one individual at the New York State Education Board has interpreted this to mean that an authorised entity licensed to provide architectural services may not associate itself with any unauthorised entity and cannot share profits or split fees with that unauthorised entity. Does this mean that firms that seek to build interdisciplinary teams, fund spatial research that contributes to other fields and actively attempt to expand the borders of the discipline of architecture will be charged with Class E felonies? Perhaps, but what can be said with certainty is that statutes such as this one, and more problematically their broad interpretation, disincentivise the very forces that are driving innovation within architecture and beyond.

In some of the most progressive and interesting offices, teams assembled to address design challenges are now constituted of much more diverse talent pools than ever before. Architecture offices not only benefit from this expanded field of practitioners, but, equally important, other fields beyond those that touch the built environment benefit from the unique perspectives, education and skills that are the product of an architectural education. It is critical that rules like this one be made relevant or removed.

Among the other regulatory constraints that deserve re-examination are the forms of prolonged apprenticeship such as the Architectural Experience Program (AXP) that frustrate entrepreneurship, as well as the strict regulation of who is allowed to use the

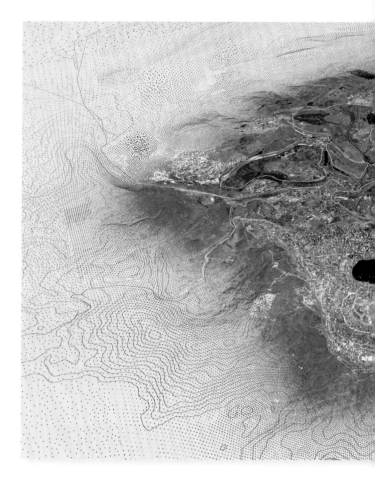

SITU Research,
Cartographic analysis and photogrammetric
reconstruction of a mine,
Cerro De Pasco,
Peru,
2019

In collaboration with Source International and Oakridge National Laboratory, a novel process was used to generate a 3D photogrammetric model of a mine in Cerro de Pasco using stereo satellite images, rendered as a point cloud with vector annotations and spatial information.

Looking at architecture in the context of the radical shifts across other industries, we can identify and isolate the statutes and regulations that alienate the 'capital A' Architect from contemporary practice

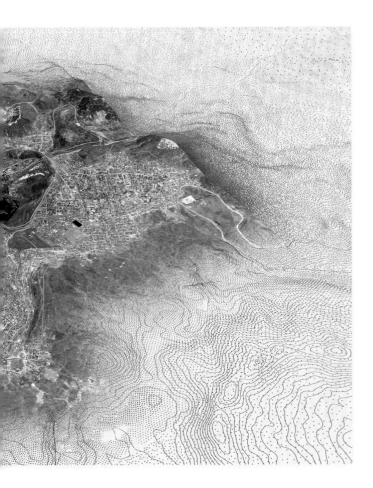

Humans have been trying to harness the power of computers to automatically generate building designs for decades. Like turning lead into gold, it seemed like a foolhardy endeavor that consumed many hopefuls. But after years of tepid results, a number of companies are finally cracking the alchemy of algorithmic space planning.[6]

The article goes on to describe the emergence of software and organisations that are finally delivering on this promise to automate building design. Examples are provided of recent work by AutoDesk subsidiary The Living, in the automated design of its own Toronto-based offices as well as an unrealised development in the Netherlands where automated processes were used to generate residential layouts. The author, Daniel Davis, goes on to quote project lead Lorenzo Villagi as saying that the manually created designs 'took an approach that was known to work based on past experience, but the algorithmic solutions moved beyond what you would typically think of'.[7] Davis hedges at the end of this article, suggesting that rather than replacing architects, the tools will proliferate the expertise of architects more widely. This reads as an effort by the author to mitigate the technological fervour and sensational language that he himself has set up.

There is little doubt that the automated processes used to generate variations for these projects led to different, and even useful, options. What is curious is the largely unqualified language used to characterise the progress this work represents. *ARCHITECT* is one of the profession's most influential outlets. Assertions of turning 'lead into gold' and 'finally cracking the alchemy of algorithmic space planning' are hyperbolic at best and very much at odds with the experience many of us have had with the relative immaturity of automated tools applied in the service of design. We remain some distance from the time when artificial intelligence and algorithmic design can provide substantive, actionable design options at the scale of an entire project. In the near term, AI is well on its way to helping us make certain decisions faster, but architects need to resist the impulse to fetishise the technology, exaggerate its development or overstate the utility of this tool.

As a discipline, we are prone to chasing shiny things – the fervour around computationally generated form that characterised much of what was happening in the Academy during the 1990s and early 2000s is a strong example in hindsight. Looking back, it is clear that the emerging tools of the time played an outsized and, at times, insidious role in shaping the pedagogy and discourse of the era.

The stakes are higher now. The over-valorisation of data as a design input brings serious risks for the contemporary moment. On the one hand it places tech companies in the driver's seat – these are corporations whose priorities, while often dressed up as prioritising social benefit, are overwhelmingly profit-driven as opposed to organisations that honestly prioritise 'the problems of living', as Rudofsky defines them.

word 'architecture' at all. In the current environment of accelerating change, arcane rules such as these will send the most talented and ambitious architects running in the opposite direction towards opportunities that promise a greater sense of agency. We are witnessing how the tech world is standing with arms outstretched to embrace disaffected young designers, offering more money, more attractive work environments and a flattened management structure that promises opportunities for increased agency.[4] Lest it become subjugated to the logics and forces of tech giants, it is essential that architecture resets some of its own rules, identity and culture.

Cautionary Tales

A counterpoint to this focus on the laws that continue to govern professional practice is the speculative and blistering rate of change of the tech sector and the ways it is shaping architectural discourse. Most conversations about the frontiers of technology and computation quickly converge on the emerging role of automation and/or artificial intelligence (AI), and any survey of how AI is rapidly gaining traction in the architecture, engineering and construction (AEC) community will yield myriad avenues for discussion. One particular text catches the eye, an article in *ARCHITECT* magazine titled 'Can Algorithms Design Buildings?'. Below the title, in large font above the body of the essay, a header reads: 'After decades of unsuccessful attempts to generate building layouts automatically, a spate of companies has suddenly proven it possible'.[5] Victory is declared! Reading on:

SITU Studio,
Cloud Pavilion,
NASA Jet Propulsion Laboratory,
Pasadena,
California,
2019

A lightweight, cellular structure, the unique form
of the Cloud Pavilion is a tessellation of folded
metal mesh tubes resting on steel columns,
which simultaneously delineates a soft, shaded
gathering area and serves as an iconic landmark for
employees and visitors alike.

Yet more importantly, we are also responsible for
protecting the built environment from overdetermination
by technocratic agendas, not simply as architects, but,
more generally, as citizens of increasingly urban
communities. As we build buildings, campuses and even
whole cities optimised for harvesting and processing data,
our default posture should be more critical than evangelical.
It is for this reason that Davis's soaring rhetoric illuminates
how we are stranded between arcane rules and fictional
presents. This is a precarious place for *ARCHITECT*
magazine, the official journal of the AIA, to occupy.

In short, we see two processes unfolding in parallel.
On the one hand, the rule-making has not kept up

SITU Studio,
New York Tech Office,
New York,
2017

above: This 3,715-square-metre (40,000-square-foot) workspace was designed for a fast-paced, multidisciplinary and intensely collaborative group. After in-depth observation of their staff and workflows, SITU Studio developed this hackable environment, rich with tech-integrated infrastructure and furniture systems that can be endlessly reconfigured to suit the diverse needs of its users.

Looking at the problems licensure addresses through this Hippocratic filter presents an opportunistic alignment with some of the saner rhetoric of automation enthusiasts who predict a future in which the toil of architecture is lessened

with the changes affecting contemporary practice. Simultaneously, claims about those changes have been vastly overstated. Taken together, architecture finds itself in a particularly vulnerable place.

A Provocation

If we remind ourselves of the nominal purpose of licensure, we come back to the AIA's stated priority: the health, safety and welfare of the public.[8] While there are, of course, other stated and unstated arguments for protecting the profession (protecting the guild, establishing norms and best practices and ethical guidelines), we can posit that the enduring function of licensure as a public good is to codify the technical yet non-creative aspects of architecture – the ability to interpret building codes, understand structural performance, and become conversant in contracts. Looking at the problems licensure addresses through this Hippocratic filter presents an opportunistic alignment with some of the saner rhetoric of automation enthusiasts who predict a future in which the toil of architecture is lessened. Through this lens, the distinction between design and compliance starts to become clearer. In an interview on the podcast Getting Simple, coder and AEC polymath Ian Keough talks about what is on the horizon:

> Like any technology, things will go away, jobs will cease to exist … the dude who used to draw that structural steel framing plan or put foundations under every column … that job will cease to exist … it is the proverbial buggy whip manufacturer … but in its place will blossom a whole bunch of other jobs and opportunities.[9]

What could this mean for the profession? If computation and automation can help ensure compliance with agreed-upon standards for public safety and building code, perhaps this is our best opportunity to refigure our relationship to the profession and shift our attention back to the 'problems of living'. Might we finally liberate architecture from Architects? ⌂

Notes
1. Bernard Rudofsky, *Architecture Without Architects: A Short Introduction to Non-Pedigreed Architecture*, Museum of Modern Art (New York), 1965, p 5.
2. *Ibid*, p 2.
3. New York State Education Department (NYSED), 'Rules of the Board of Regents', 5 October 2011: www.op.nysed.gov/title8/part29.htm.
4. Anne Quito, 'WeWork is Retraining a Generation of Architects to Think in Terms of Data', *Metropolis*, 25 February 2019: www.metropolismag.com/architecture/workplace-architecture/wework-workplace-design-data-analytics/.
5. Daniel Davis, 'Can Algorithms Design Buildings?', *ARCHITECT*, 24 June 2019: www.architectmagazine.com/technology/can-algorithms-design-buildings_o.
6. *Ibid*.
7. *Ibid*.
8. American Institute of Architects (AIA), 'Where We Stand: Professional Licensure', 25 January 2018: www.aia.org/press-releases/175051-where-we-stand-professional-licensure.
9. 'Ian Keough – How to Make Better Decisions Faster', Getting Simple podcast, 1 August 2018: https://gettingsimple.com/ian-keough.

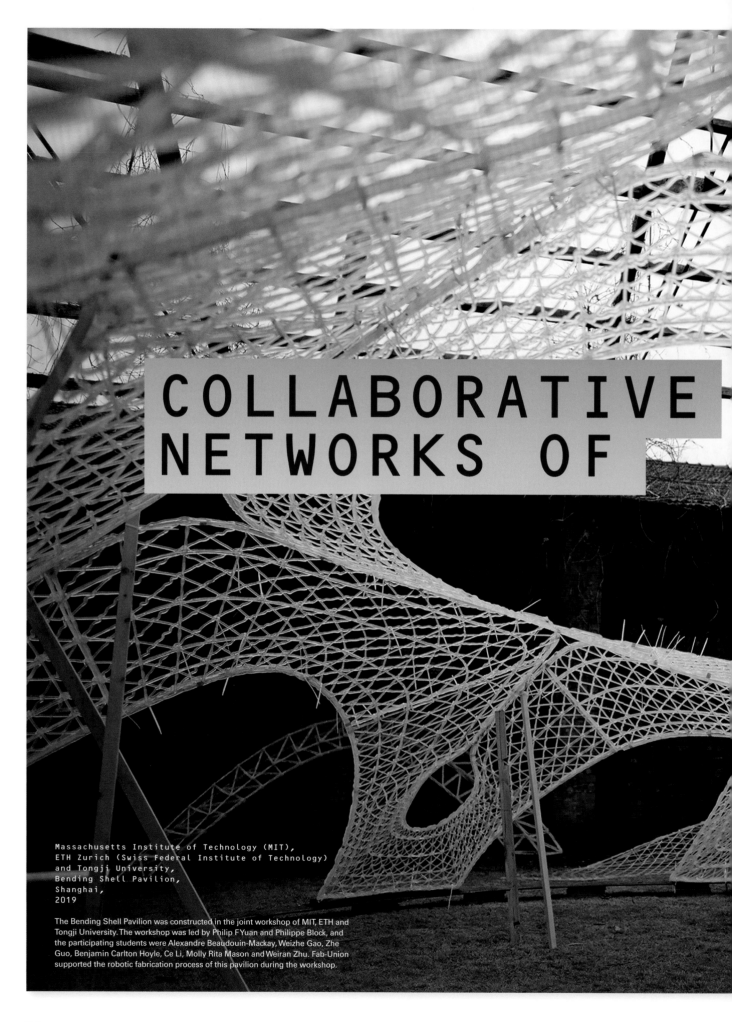

COLLABORATIVE NETWORKS OF

Massachusetts Institute of Technology (MIT),
ETH Zurich (Swiss Federal Institute of Technology)
and Tongji University,
Bending Shell Pavilion,
Shanghai,
2019

The Bending Shell Pavilion was constructed in the joint workshop of MIT, ETH and Tongji University. The workshop was led by Philip F Yuan and Philippe Block, and the participating students were Alexandre Beaudouin-Mackay, Weizhe Gao, Zhe Guo, Benjamin Carlton Hoyle, Ce Li, Molly Rita Mason and Weiran Zhu. Fab-Union supported the robotic fabrication process of this pavilion during the workshop.

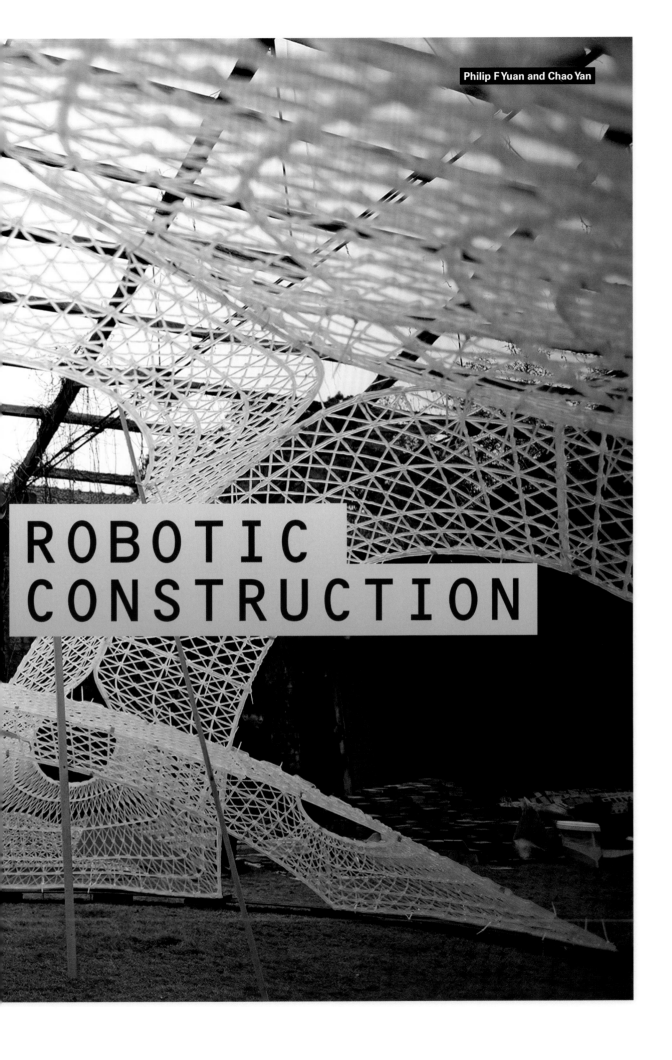

Philip F Yuan and Chao Yan

ROBOTIC
CONSTRUCTION

Constructing architecture today is a matter of many parallel dialogues between humanity and machines. **Professor Philip F Yuan** and postdoctoral researcher **Chao Yan**, of Tongji University, discuss the products and aspirations of Shanghai-based Archi-Union Architects and Fab-Union Technology, founded by Yuan, and their search for ever more dynamic communication between them and their digitally enabled, robotic co-workers.

Over the last 20 years, digital technology has cultivated a significant paradigm shift in architectural research and practice. New tools for architectural design and construction have been constantly invented and reinvented under human–machine collaborations, seeking new ways of conception and realisation of complex forms.

In recent years, scholars such as Antoine Picon and Mario Carpo have devoted themselves to this technological transformation in architecture, trying to redefine the notion of the architect and its role in the social and political context from a theoretical and historical standpoint.[1]

In correspondence with these theoretical enquiries, the Shanghai-based Archi-Union design institute and Fab-Union robotic factory have been collaborating closely with each other, inventing and applying advanced digital tools such as library-based robotic software and robotics-aided fabrication techniques in their architectural research and practice over the last 15 years. By pursuing innovations in the building system, they seek to transform the architectural discipline and upgrade its industry practice on the basis of new human-to-human collaborations.

REDEFINING THE ARCHITECT
AS MASTER BUILDER

From research-based design to research-based practice, the scope of exploration of digital technology in contemporary architecture has now extended to the whole process of design and construction. This is reflected by the emergence of digital fabrication labs around the world, such as the National Centre of Competence in Research (NCCR) lab at ETH Zurich (the Swiss Federal Institute of Technology), and the Institute for Computational Design and Construction (ICD) at Stuttgart University. As one of these labs, Fab-Union has also been seeking ways to integrate the design-to-construction process. In its collaboration with the Archi-Union design institute, one of the main goals is to redefine the architect as master builder in the digital era.

From ancient times to the Middle Ages, buildings were built by artisans, craftsmen and the master builders working on the construction site. Since the Renaissance, drawing as the notational tool has separated the architect from the construction process.[2] Later, through divisions of labour in the modern era, on-site building construction was replaced by industrial prefabrication and assembly lines. These evolutions have resulted in a deskilling situation where architects have gradually lost the knowledge and skills of building construction.

By combining industrial robots with digital design software as a revolutionary construction platform, we can now see a clear transformation of architectural production, from traditional crafts and industrial reproduction to a new craftsmanship of the digital age. With the combination of digital design tools and architectural robotics, customised components can be built through numerically controlled processes, and the industrial standardisation of mass-produced products can be fundamentally reimagined.

More importantly, these tools not only improve the dynamicity of communication between design and construction, but also provide new possibilities for creation. In this human–machine collaboration, the relationship between architects and construction is once again closely connected. However, the construction machine is not only a tool of making, but also a tool of thinking. The tools and processes of design-to-construction itself can be a source of creation. Applications of digital tools and robots are not limited to visualisation and realisation of the conceived form by human subjects, but can be involved directly in the creative process itself. In design, no longer is the human the only author of an architectural project. Machines are also part of the design subject, forming a new subjective in the creation process. In this way, the new possibilities of collaboration between human and machine challenge traditional design authorship and question authority within the cycle of architectural design and construction.[3]

This new mode of architectural production will be fundamentally different from the process of design–draw–build. Through human–machine collaboration, the object-centred production model undergoes a significant transformation. In contemporary practice, many architects seem to focus more on inventing new tools and procedures instead of formal languages and styles. Shifting this focus could result in radically new scenarios of architectural authorship and ownership. Architects are not only credited for offering building designs, but also the tools producing them.[4]

TOOLKITS: MACHINE, SOFTWARE, CRAFT
With this new mode of architectural production, Archi-Union and Fab-Union have been devoting themselves to the exploration of new tools for both architectural research and practice. By establishing the partnership with the Digital Design Research Center (DDRC) of Tongji University, Archi-Union and Fab-Union set up the laboratory to conduct a series of research projects related to digital design, robotic construction, human–computer interaction etc. In 2012, Fab-Union assisted the DDRC of Tongji University to set up an architectural robot laboratory on the campus, building a collaborative dual-robot fabrication platform. Later, in November 2015, Fab-Union, Archi-Union and the DDRC together built the world's first gantry dual-robot construction platform. During the same period, from 2012 to 2018, Fab-Union, Archi-Union and the DDRC also collaborated to develop a series of in-situ robotic construction platforms.

In parallel to the hardware tools, Fab-Union has additionally been developing software platforms in order to seamlessly bridge design and construction. FuRobot is one of the well-developed tools of the last few years. As an open-ended robotic programming platform, FuRobot seeks to establish a design–construction feedback loop on the programming end, in order to achieve the flexibility to produce the customised component in prefabrication or to respond to the uncertain environment in in-situ construction.

Furthermore, on the basis of the software and hardware, crafts are also defined as the virtual toolkits being explored in Fab-Union's research. Crafts could be interpreted as particular ways of interacting with matter in the traditional sense. With the nostalgic association with craft,[5] Fab-Union has been trying to integrate traditional construction methods with new digital technologies, translating crafts into design procedures with a particular relationship to algorithms, robotic technologies and materials – such as 3D timber assembly, carbon-fibre winding, 3D metal printing and 3D plastic printing.

In association with machine, software and craft, the design–construction feedback loop involves a collaborative relationship between architect and tools to constantly form and reform design intent. Design intent is no longer solely preconceived by the architect, but is derived from the particular way of using tools. A design can now be conceived and reconceived at any stage of the design-to-construction process, producing a dynamic workflow of formation, simulation, iteration, optimisation and fabrication. For example, in the wound carbon-fibre footbridge completed in 2019, the optimal curve shape of the bridge profile was generated by the

Fab-Union,
In-situ construction robot,
2018

The in-situ robotic platform was developed by Fab-Union in order to deal with more complex scenarios at construction sites.

structural form-finding algorithm at the formation stage; then at the simulation stage the relationship between the structural performance and the bridge profile was reconsidered and revised in accordance with the material properties; and lastly the form of the bridge was modified again, taking the specific techniques of the robotic fabrication process into account.

In an integrated design-to-construction process, data transfer between the architect and various tools can form a networked feedback relationship across production stages. The introduction of multiple tools constitutes a multi-objective design model, which in turn will reciprocate feedback on modifications of design intent. The architect always maintains a collaborative relationship with the machine, forming an augmented design subject.

Fab-Union and the Digital Design Research Center (DDRC) of Tongji University, Robotically printed plastic bridge, Shanghai, 2017

Fab-Union has been collaborating with the DDRC of Tongji University to conduct annual research projects on bridges. The aim of these projects is to test various fabrication techniques on different materials. The robotically printed plastic bridge integrates a stratified printing technique of modified plastic with a robotic platform.

Fab-Union and the Digital Design Research Center (DDRC) of Tongji University, Robotically printed metal bridge, Shanghai, 2018

The robotically printed metal bridge applies robotic 3D printing techniques to the construction of a steel structure.

Fab-Union and the Digital Design Research Center (DDRC) of Tongji University, Robotically wound fibre bridge, Shanghai, 2019

The robotically wound fibre bridge develops a particular tool for carbon-fibre winding on a robotic platform.

COLLABORATIVE PLATFORM

Human–machine collaborative production relies on software and hardware platforms. These platforms can in turn form the basis for new human-to-human collaborations. The most obvious examples are information integration tools such as building information modelling (BIM), which can be used as a collaborative platform to reorganise the network of designers, builders, engineers, and experts from other disciplines. With this understanding, the current exploration of digital technologies has also begun to gradually move beyond the mere pursuit of realising algorithm-generated complex forms, turning to challenging the traditional organisation of the architectural industry.

In this context, Archi-Union and Fab-Union have been embracing the culture of the open-source in the digital age, continuing to build collaborative platforms with a special focus on the production of knowledge in architecture. The machine, the software and the craft can all be interpreted as the open-source production platform, within which anyone can contribute and share knowledge. In this way, the authorship/ownership of both the tool itself and the method of using it could be decentralised to form a dynamic way of knowledge production.

Here, the meaning of 'platform' refers not only to the actual networks of collaboration, but also to knowledge-sharing communities. By building robotic construction factories, new possibilities of collaboration among digital fabrication laboratories around the world have emerged, creating a social community that shares common interests in exploring new tools, materials, techniques and processes of experimental construction. The physical platform is interwoven with this dynamic community of laboratories, driving knowledge production for architectural construction.

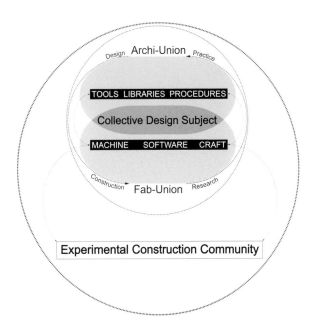

Philip F Yuan and Chao Yan,
Diagram of the collaboration of Fab-Union and Archi-Union,
2019

Fab-Union and Archi-Union have been collaborating with each other to form feedback loops between design and construction, and between research and practice. The research platform they have established on machine, software and craft also forms collaborative relationships with other laboratories.

By building robotic construction factories, new possibilities of collaboration among digital fabrication laboratories around the world have emerged

Fab-Union,
Robotic factory,
Shanghai,
2015

The robotic factory was designed and constructed by Fab-Union in order to conduct design-to-construction research projects.

Knowledge sharing and research collaboration among laboratories challenges traditional authorship and authority in knowledge production within the cycle of architectural research and practice. The essential transformation of knowledge production is reflected in the dynamic collaborating mechanisms of workshops, international conferences, exhibitions, academic associations, guest-teaching posts and so on. These diversified collaborations construct dynamic social relationships among scholars and can potentially drive new research directions for construction technology. Meanwhile, due to differing cultural backgrounds, regional policies and social pursuits, there are also certain differences of research procedure that distinguish laboratories around the world. In pursuing a common research interest that is cultivated in the social network of the scholars' community, each laboratory can have a highly personalised methodology for the research process. In the end, tensions between the common research interest and the differentiated research process will form a highly dynamic network of knowledge production and cultivate fluxes in the technological iteration of building construction.

Fab-Union has been supporting the DigitalFUTURES workshops in Shanghai since 2011. Through an annual digital fabrication workshop and international conference, top universities and research institutes including ICD Stuttgart, ETH Zurich and others have come together to explore the possibilities of digital design and fabrication technology for upgrading of the construction system. Through close collaboration and knowledge sharing with these organisations, Fab-Union has been developing new digital tools, construction platforms and fabrication techniques that have the potential to be applied to larger-scale, complex buildings. These research outcomes can be directly applied in the works of the Archi-Union design institute, thereby contributing to contemporary professional architectural practice.

Massachusetts Institute of Technology (MIT),
ETH Zurich (Swiss Federal Institute of Technology)
and Tongji University,
Bending Shell Pavilion,
Shanghai,
2019

The robotic plastic printing mould for the pavilion was designed in a particular geometry so that it could be robotically printed as a flat sheet, and then folded into spatial form for the shell construction.

Archi-Union Architects,
Inkstone House OCT
Linpan Cultural Center,
Sichuan Province,
2018

right: Robotic construction tools were applied to the local context to reinvent the traditional crafts for the construction of the floating roof.

opposite: The curved roof geometry with traditional ceramic tiles was precisely constructed through an integrated design-to-construction process.

PLURAL SUBJECTS IN DESIGN/CONSTRUCTION PRACTICE

Today, with shared tools, libraries and procedures, architecture has become a collective endeavour, in which not only is design intent collectively formed, but also architectural knowledge is produced by decentralised networks of scholars. Within the collaborative platform, as Benjamin Bratton argues, '[the user's] own intelligence is networked with the platform and with the wider collective of robotic and human users with whom it collaborates.'[6] In that sense, the subject of architectural production would become plural in the social dimension.

In his book *Laboratory Life*, first published in 1979, Bruno Latour challenges the distinction between the social and intellectual dimensions of science, particularly proposing questions on the causal relationship between social networks and scientific pursuits: 'does the formation of social groupings give rise to the pursuit by scientists of certain intellectual lines of enquiry, or does the existence of intellectual problems lead to the creation of social networks of scientists?'[7] Now, in architecture, the social nature of technological development in the design-to-construction process brings alternative perspectives to the production of architectural knowledge within the dynamic correlations between scholars, practitioners, laboratories and technology itself. As pioneers of these new modes of practice, how can architects actively participate in collaboration-based knowledge production and, in so doing, rethink the social significance of technological innovation in building construction? Archi-Union and Fab-Union will continue to investigate and discuss these essential issues through research and practice collaborations.[8] ᴆ

Notes
1. See Mario Carpo, *The Alphabet and the Algorithm*, MIT Press (Cambridge, MA), 2001; Wendy W Fok and Antoine Picon (eds), ᴆ *Digital Property: Open-Source Architecture*, September/October (no 5), 2016.
2. Robin Evans, *The Projective Cast: Architecture and Its Three Geometries*, MIT Press (Cambridge, MA), 2000, pp 113–21.
3. Carpo, *The Alphabet and the Algorithm, op cit,* p 117.
4. Antoine Picon, 'From Authorship to Ownership', in Wendy W Fok and Antoine Picon (eds), ᴆ *Digital Property: Open-Source Architecture*, September/October (no 5), 2016, pp 36–41.
5. Antoine Picon, 'Digital Fabrication, Between Disruption and Nostalgia', in Chandler Ahrens and Aaron Sprecher (eds), *Instabilities and Potentialities: Notes on the Nature of Knowledge in Digital Architecture*, Routledge (New York), 2019, pp 221–36.
6. Benjamin H Bratton, *The Stack: On Software and Sovereignty,* MIT Press (Cambridge, MA), 2015, pp 134–40.
7. Bruno Latour and Steve Woolgar, *Laboratory Life: The Construction of Scientific Facts,* Princeton University Press (Princeton, NJ), 1986, pp 11–23.
8. This article is funded by the Special Funds for State Key R&D Programme during the 13th Five-Year Plan Period of China (Grant No 2016YFC0702104), the National Natural Science Foundation of China (Grant No 51578378) and the Sino-German Center Research Project (Grant No GZ1162).

The Distractions of Disruptions

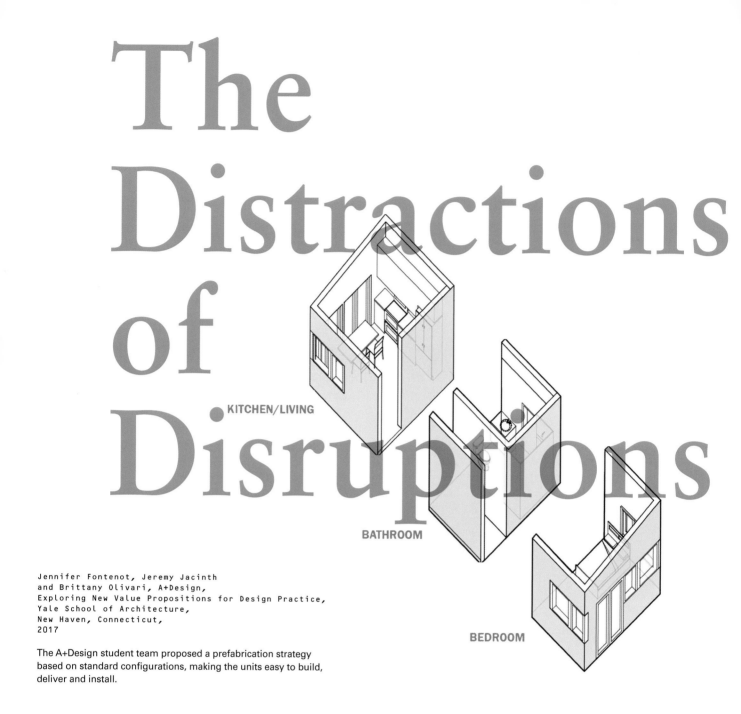

KITCHEN/LIVING

BATHROOM

BEDROOM

Jennifer Fontenot, Jeremy Jacinth
and Brittany Olivari, A+Design,
Exploring New Value Propositions for Design Practice,
Yale School of Architecture,
New Haven, Connecticut,
2017

The A+Design student team proposed a prefabrication strategy
based on standard configurations, making the units easy to build,
deliver and install.

Architect and Associate Dean at the Yale School of
Architecture, **Phil Bernstein** sees a tsunami of change
brewing for the architectural profession, conditioned by
artificial intelligence, big data, the ubiquitous cloud and
robotics. Yet the delivery and procurement of buildings
is often inhibited by pre-digital structures of the
construction industry. He argues that architects need
to rethink their processes from first principles.

Phil Bernstein

Technical Supply in an Era of Social Demand

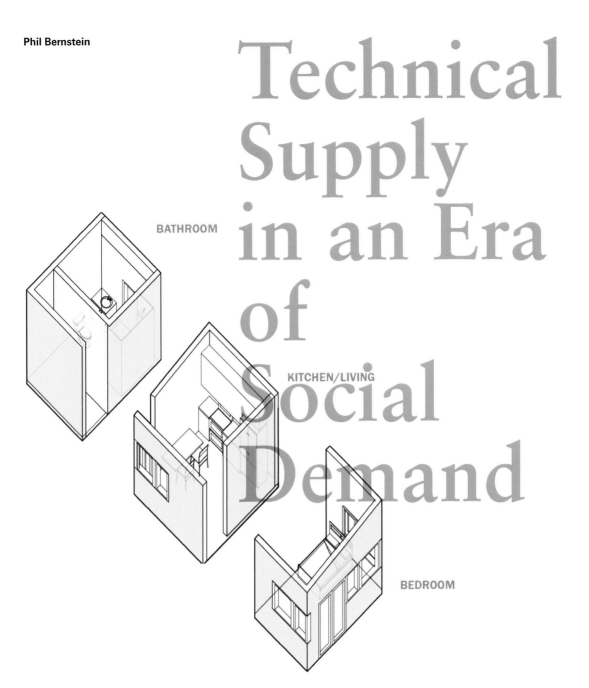

BATHROOM

KITCHEN/LIVING

BEDROOM

In the spring of 2013, a new course was offered at the Yale School of Architecture, one of only two in its professional practice curriculum. Exploring New Value Propositions for Design Practice was a small seminar designed to interrogate current business models, examine other models both within and outside of the building industry, and propose new strategies for the practice of architecture. Its first students had vivid memories of the recent world financial crisis, and despite the relative isolation caused by studio-based design education they were very much aware of the general 'startup' zeitgeist among their peers on college campuses elsewhere. Since that first trial run, the course has grown in popularity and size as one of few opportunities for architects-in-training to experiment beyond the boundaries of building design in the innovation era.

The expanding interest in the course is a product of a general questioning of the efficacy of traditional practice among today's generation of students. Having experienced the worst downturn in modern history, and saddled with the daunting financial obligations of paying for a graduate education in the US, students seem far more engaged in questions of professional efficacy and economics than their peers of even a decade ago. Traditional design education – and its aesthetic solutions – seems hardly up to the challenges of globalisation, emergent nationalism, climate change and income inequality. Architects need new approaches and new tools – not just software – and thus interest in startup culture reaches beyond mere economic self-interest.

Adventures in Disruption

Architecture's early forays into disruptive technologies have certainly not been up to such giant challenges. Having experienced two relatively mild digital transformations in the past two decades – first computer-aided design (CAD), then building information modelling (BIM) – design practice, as a part of the larger construction industry, is likely to see true digital disruption over the next 20 years. While those working within those first two waves may have struggled to keep their professional heads above water (and certainly both the technologies absorbed felt dramatic at the time), the change was largely limited to the creation, management and production of representational information, primarily in the form of two-dimensional drawing. While CAD (and, to a lesser extent, scripting) brought us some formal exuberance, and BIM the tantalising prospect of data-driven design, contractors viewing a BIM-generated PDF on their iPads while on construction sites is much more a convenience than a disruption. That the drawing they are using is relatively free of construction coordination errors seems like a small-bore victory.

But there are two strong indicators that the real disruption in building may be upon us, brought by the Cloud, big data, machine learning or artificial intelligence – the stuff one sees advertised in every international airport today, despite architecture's currently limited exposure to or use thereof. The first is the digital transformation of clients' processes: those on the demand side of the building equation are increasingly using these technologies to run their enterprises, particularly in finance, medicine and certainly across the corporate spectrum. They are learning to use data, analysis and simulation to develop the business case for building and ultimately run their businesses themselves. As the work of clients becomes more data-driven, the business of architects will have to follow suit.

The second sign of a coming tsunami is signalled by the chosen consultants of the neoliberal economy, McKinsey, who produced several reports about the digital and productivity opportunities of the digitisation of construction[1] and its productivity (or lack thereof).[2] These studies systematically restate the obvious: construction is desperately under-digitised, and productivity growth is negative. The building industry, being laggard, is therefore an excellent target for investment by McKinsey's venture capital clients, portending a wave of investment in technology in support of design, construction and building operation. In fact, since 2017 billions have flowed into architecture, engineering and construction (AEC) tech startups, including Japan's Softbank investment in Katerra, Autodesk's purchase of PlanGrid, and the emergence of AEC-specific venture funds. With all this new capital, where are the opportunities, and what might they mean for the changing roles of architects and practice?

Today's students are certainly primed for such changes. To be educated as an architect now is to be steeped in fundamental optimism for the potential for change: introduced to a series of provocative technologies (digital modelling, fabrication, scripting, virtual reality); trained to solve complex, ambiguous problems; and convinced of the efficacy of the built environment to help solve those problems. But are the platforms of professional practice – business and delivery models and their related value propositions – up to the task?

Testing the Limits of the Design Business Model

The ultimate goal for Yale's Exploring New Value students is to take their newfound understanding of the limitations of the operating model of practice and propose a business that leverages their skills as architects to create new value propositions and, by definition, opportunities to make money. Experimenting on simple spreadsheets, they first explore and then test the limits of profitability typical of the traditional practice operating model. Profit is not an exclusive objective of the work, but rather a proxy for improving the value of architects' services. Architects are fond of asserting the value of their work, but fail to convert those assertions into actual money, thus profitability becomes a proof point for the proposals.

With the help of a group of experienced management consultants who school them in the performance parameters of successful firms (and characteristics of financial failures) as well as the mechanics of business model design, students rapidly grasp the realities of the commoditised fixed-fee business model. There are scant options for making a practice more profitable when compensation is so limited: either get bigger fees, or produce work more efficiently. As there are only two dials on this particular machine to adjust, it is easy to convince them to consider abandoning the model altogether.

Phil Bernstein,
Practice business
model structure,
2019

The diagram illustrates the flow of project funds through a firm's operating model, starting at the top with the conversion of suspect (possible) projects, to prospect (shortlisted) project to actual work with fees. Project compensation filters down through various uses until the remainder is channelled into profits or working capital.

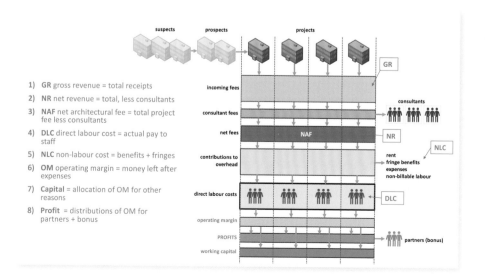

1) **GR** gross revenue = total receipts
2) **NR** net revenue = total, less consultants
3) **NAF** net architectural fee = total project fee less consultants
4) **DLC** direct labour cost = actual pay to staff
5) **NLC** non-labour cost = benefits + fringes
6) **OM** operating margin = money left after expenses
7) **Capital** = allocation of OM for other reasons
8) **Profit** = distributions of OM for partners + bonus

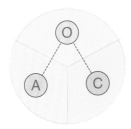

Phil Bernstein,
Delivery Relationships,
2019

The basic relationship between
owners (O), architects (A) and
contractors (C) that is the key
to the strategic analysis of
information and value flows
between the players.

Phil Bernstein,
Spanning strategies,
Exploring New Value
Propositions for
Design Practice,
Yale School of
Architecture,
New Haven,
Connecticut,
2019

A few ambitious teams took
on ideas that connected any
two adjacent components
of the delivery chain
to provide services not
usually undertaken in pure
design, such as artificial
intelligence support for
design to construction, or
post-occupancy evaluation
datasets then sold to architects
for reference on subsequent
projects.

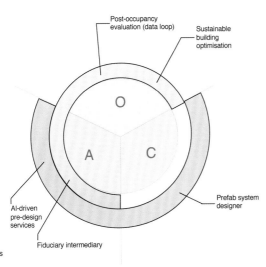

Phil Bernstein,
Verticalisation
strategies,
Exploring New Value
Propositions for
Design Practice,
Yale School of
Architecture,
New Haven,
Connecticut,
2019

Eleven of the student projects
were based on architects
assuming a different role in
the supply chain, from specific
responsibilities as developer or
fabricator, to complete control
as an integrated design/build/
operate entity.

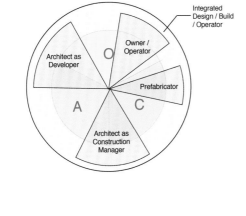

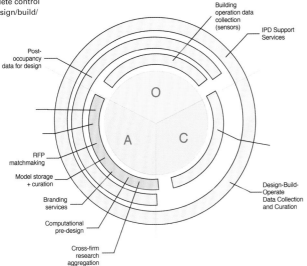

Phil Bernstein,
Augmenting the Delivery Chain,
Exploring New Value Propositions
for Design Practice,
Yale School of Architecture,
New Haven, Connecticut,
2019

The majority of projects focused on specific 'value
added' services to augment the core service
provided by architects. Several proposals included
multidisciplinary services to provide alternative
delivery consulting or data management and
coordination.

Directions of Disruption

Over the six terms the course has been taught, more than 50
proposals for such businesses have been produced, and while
this sample is hardly exhaustive nor even statistically valid (as
it likely reflects some of the prejudices of the instructor setting
up the problem), some clear categories of ideas have emerged.
Together, these are a useful strategic taxonomy for looking at
potential disruptions in the business models of practice, and
a likely guide for both the directions of practice and certain
entrepreneurial architects.

The first strategy is 'spanning', where a firm extends or
redefines the range of services architects provide, expanding
these beyond the typical core model of design and production:
taking responsibility for what might traditionally be called
'additional services' in feasibility studies, pre-design or
during construction, or converting typical commoditised fee
approaches to performance-based alternatives.

A second approach could be called 'verticalising',
expanding the scope of control to construction or ownership
and assuming the role of client (usually a developer) and/
or sub-contractor or constructor, and thus becoming both
provider and consumer of the architect's services.

Finally, a more catch-all category is 'augmenting', where
the firm provides necessary adjacent services or software to the
industry. This includes an array of extra-mural consultancies
or software products aimed at increasing design potential
by providing enhanced capabilities such as digitised tools
(databases or other supporting instruments) to architects or
others in the delivery chain.

Mapping the variety of projects accordingly is instructive
in the sense that it is a rough measure of both the students'
nascent understanding of the needs/opportunities of the
profession and their interests. If this limited cohort is any
indication, the next generation wish to move far beyond
traditional practice, and potential disruptions from within
the profession may largely derive from their rising unease
about normative practice models. They doubt the efficacy
of old-school firms, see working in them only as a means to
obtain licensure, and plan to find their own way, through
new models, as soon as they are properly certified. A small
but significant number are obtaining MBAs in concert with
their design degrees; interestingly, these candidates have the
most difficulty finding work in traditional firms, who have no
idea how to properly employ their otherwise highly desirable
combined skills.

Jennifer Fontenot, Jeremy Jacinth
and Brittany Olivari, A+Design,
Exploring New Value Propositions
for Design Practice,
Yale School of Architecture,
New Haven, Connecticut,
2017

This student project proposes a solution for ageing-in-place housing that exploits zoning regulations in Seattle that allow auxiliary housing units to be built on single-family sites as-of-right. It combines three strategies: design, construction and installation of prefabricated extra units, rented Airbnb-style until the family owning the property wishes to downsize, at which time they sell the main house and move into the auxiliary unit.

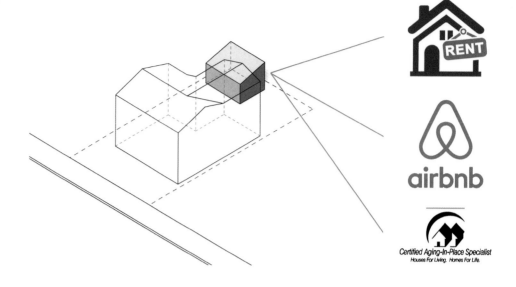

Exploded view of an auxiliary unit. Part of A+Design's value proposition was design configurations based on the use of local materials, with a wide palette of options for individual customers to create a bespoke unit.

CHOOSE YOUR HOME, CUSTOMIZE YOUR FINISHES, ALL LOCALLY SOURCED

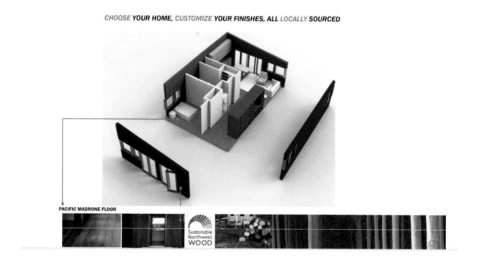

PACIFIC MADRONE FLOOR

Sustainable Northwest WOOD

BUSINESS MODEL

SUPPLIERS — INNOVATION HUB (IN-HOUSE) — CONSUMERS

FOR-PROFIT MODEL

CROSS-LAMINATED TIMBER

PANELLISED CONSTRUCTION SYSTEMS

BUILDING MATERIAL INDUSTRY - CONTRACTORS

AGRO WASTE

CULTURING MYCELIUM

LICENSED INTELLECTUAL PROPERTY

FUNDING THROUGH COMPANY MODEL AS A NON-PROFIT

Dhruvin Shah and Colin Sutherland,
Mycelium-based building product
manufacturer business plan,
Exploring New Value Propositions
for Design Practice,
Yale School of Architecture,
New Haven, Connecticut,
2019

In conjunction with an advanced design studio examining new models for building products based on renewable sources, the student team proposed a business plan based on sourcing and fabricating cross-laminated timber (CLT) modules and prefabricated panels created from mycelium plants.

Turning the Direction of Practice

If nothing else, these young architects will bring to their first professional experiences a potentially disruptive combination of extreme digital skills and the entrepreneurial zeal of the WeWork generation. But will this be enough to catalyse sufficient change to maintain their interest in and commitment to the field? And will they remain in the profession long enough to see the changes through? Widespread adoption of the most recent technological upheaval in design – BIM – took almost two decades.

The groundswell of startup technology companies competing to digitise the building industry will surely tempt many such talented young architects away from mainstream practice, and this may well serve the profession well in the long run, as until now it has largely been the recipient, rather than the creator, of new technologies. But it will be equally important for some of these entrepreneurs to remain with traditional firms and transform them from within. The second digital turn will inevitably bring data-driven processes to the discipline of design, and with them entirely new protocols for how buildings are formulated, resolved, detailed and produced. Algorithms will replace rote procedures; information flows from the control systems of running buildings will inform the design of their successors; machine learning programs will study the digital representations of multiple designs and infer best practices from them. There are great opportunities to radically improve the work of architects, and great dangers that they may replace our work altogether. Only architects themselves can define their routes towards new definitions of practice, and it is these students – and not their 'baby boomer' predecessors currently practising and teaching – who must lead the way.

In *The Second Digital Turn: Design Beyond Intelligence* (2017), Mario Carpo reminds us (quoting the work of anthropologist André Leroi-Gourhan) that 'every technology is a social construction: innovation only occurs when technical supply meets social demand'.[3] The entrepreneurial opportunity in architecture lies in bridging the gulf between the two. Architecture is a part of larger building delivery systems that, while embracing technology now, are far from having taken full advantage of the tools currently available, much less the looming potential of the coming generation of data-driven, machine-learning-enabled technologies. Today's architecture students will be mid-career practitioners by the time we can reasonably expect the industry to have understood, implemented and potentially transformed through artificial intelligence. Let us hope they are optimistic and patient enough to guide those changes to their potentially transformative ends. ∆

Notes
1. Mckinsey Global Institute, *Solving the Productivity Puzzle: The Role of Demand and the Promise of Digitization*, February 2018: www.mckinsey.com/~/media/mckinsey/featured%20insights/meeting%20societys%20expectations/solving%20the%20productivity%20puzzle/mg-solving-the-productivity-puzzle--report-february-2018.ashx.
2. Mckinsey Global Institute, *Reinventing Construction: A Route to Higher Productivity*, February 2017: https://www.mckinsey.com/~/media/McKinsey/Industries/Capital%20Projects%20and%20Infrastructure/Our%20Insights/Reinventing%20construction%20through%20a%20productivity%20revolution/MGI-Reinventing-Construction-Executive-summary.ashx.
3. Mario Carpo, *The Second Digital Turn: Design Beyond Intelligence*, MIT Press (Cambridge, MA), 2017, p 159.

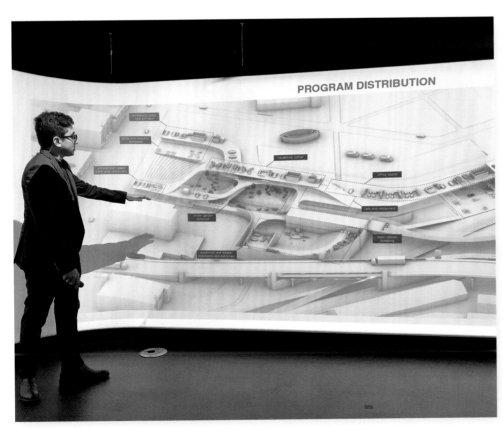

Dhruvin Shah and Colin Sutherland with Kunhee Chang, Innovation hub for new building materials, Exploring New Value Propositions for Design Practice, Yale School of Architecture, New Haven, Connecticut, 2019

Student designer and class participant Dhruvin Shah presents a solution for an innovation hub for new building materials. The building design was created in an advanced studio taught by Professors Anna Dyson and Chris Sharples.

Jared Della Valle

Better
Development
Alternative
Value Creation

Alloy,
John Street Pasture,
Brooklyn, New York City,
2014

A field of crimson clover was installed in the future location of One John Street. Goats were utilised to eat the clover prior to the interim park's removal.

How can urban development help address the social inequities within our cities? Alloy, a socially responsible architecture and real-estate firm based in Brooklyn, New York, invests in its locality, has developed a 'Swiss-army-knife' multivalent, flat staffing structure and is its own client. **Jared Della Valle,** CEO and founder, describes its strategies.

Alloy operates under a different model of practice – one that takes on a small number of projects in a focused community and performs comprehensive building delivery functions on each, from site acquisition and financing through design and construction, and into sales and building management. This singular responsibility for the project across all phases gives the firm, based in Brooklyn, New York, a very different business model and a unique level of control over how and why it undertakes projects. It is a model that impacts everything from the way staff are organised to the financing of operations.

The practice started based on the principals' frustrations with the architectural profession, an ambition to have greater control of the project and a desire to make their own decisions. The motivation was also about capturing the tangible value of intellectual property created by design, against the actual asset value, which is not at all how architects are compensated as a profession.

Alloy has morphed into a group of principals that care more about the *intangible* value of each project – the ability to leverage control of its tangible value to make decisions impacting the cultural, aesthetic and other social values of building. The tangible economic value is necessary in order to execute the work, but the outcomes are judged by intangibles: Is the project memorable? How does it influence people? How does it perform and relate in its context? And

what other values can projects bring to bear? Alloy has the potential to create this intangible value through its work. Because Alloy is the developer, it gets to articulate, determine and prioritise when it chooses to invest and on what. Alloy gets to drive programme so it can determine whether there are other social or political values that it wants to achieve.

This places the firm squarely between the value of architects who dream about creating public space or buildings of civic importance, and developers who think about creating valuable economic outcomes with the building as a vehicle. Being in the middle of these value propositions means that Alloy is much more deliberate about where and when to acquire a property and invest both economic and intellectual capital.

Team and Project Organisation
Alloy is a partnership, organised with Alloy Development Holdings taking on sole responsibility for its projects. Along with investors, Alloy invests in and owns a project-specific entity which in turn owns the project. This project-level entity retains Alloy Advisory for real-estate brokerage services, Alloy Design for full architectural services, and a project-specific construction entity for construction management services that is sometimes owned by Alloy Construction. Once complete, the property retains Alloy Management for ongoing building services. Company overheads are divided annually by each service model's proportionate share of revenue through a resource-sharing agreement. All agreements are industry-standard arm's-length agreements and utilised to conform to licensure requirements, and to segregate expenses for Alloy's partners and lenders. Remarkably, this leads to situations where the same principal signs change orders and requisitions as owner, contractor and architect, effectively collapsing the responsibility of a project's success to a single entity.

Legend:
— Ownership
■ ■ ■ ■ Service Agreement (AIA Documents, B141, A133, A201)
▪ ▪ ▪ ▪ Resource Sharing Agreement

Alloy,
Business organisational model,
2019

Alloy's company and project organisation. The firm sets up a number of single-project subsidiaries to cover the roles performed across each project.

Alloy,
Firm value creation model,
2019

Traditional architect vs Alloy project value models. The
traditional architectural service model can only generate
profit as a margin on services hours. Alloy's model is
diversified across multiple value-creation activities.

Architecture Practice

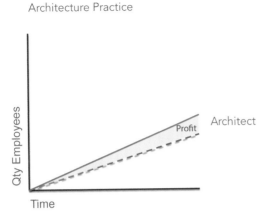

Diversified Practice

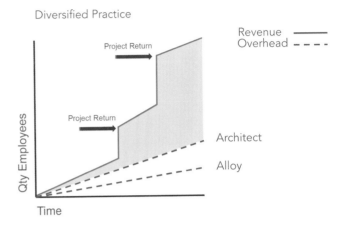

Firm Composition

The traditional architecture firm's business model is typical to any professional services company: it is pyramidal – with partners managing a pyramid of increasingly junior staff. As a partner, the more people you have working for you, the more services you can sell and the more money you can make provided you can manage the time spent against the time billed. In all instances the architectural model limits the revenue to margin on employee hours; there are limited other revenue sources. This context creates an incentive to grow by taking on more staff, to the point where cyclical project or economic forces can cause firms to churn employees as projects start and stop.

The composition of Alloy's employees – where they work and what they do – is different because they are involved across all aspects of making a building. There are moments when staff are all working on development, or on design, and others where everyone is working on construction or brokerage. This makes Alloy feel as though its team is bigger than it actually is, because everyone has a Swiss-army-knife kind of capacity. Each individual participates throughout the process, which makes the work varied and enjoyable. Within the last 10 years Alloy has completed only five projects, all of which have been within a block of the office.

In Alloy's business model there is dramatically less volatility than in traditional architecture firms. Over the course of a project, Alloy pays itself architecture fees, development fees, construction fees if it is the contractor, and brokerage fees if it is the real-estate broker. These fees add up to approximately 20 per cent of the total project cost. Alloy has the ability to do the same project with fewer people, eliminating the need to build a big pyramid. Being the owner also brings an ability to control the project

schedule so that the total quantity of staff need not fluctuate. Alloy staff are on average more highly skilled than in a standard architectural practice. Of the 15 people who have architectural training, eight are licensed architects. It would not make sense for a traditional architectural practice to run that top heavy. Project time and the cost of staff are important to the model; however, preserving institutional knowledge is more valuable than short-term profit for Alloy. Because the firm is not limited by the value of architectural services alone, it is not constrained by the amount of time spent documenting its buildings, which in turn helps mitigate professional liability and project risk for Alloy and its partners.

Alloy's revenue model is not solely based on margin on top of staff. In addition to service margins, Alloy has a major stake in the future value of the project. When a project is completed, Alloy gets to share in all proceeds over and above the actual costs with its partners. Unfortunately, the market determines what can be charged for architectural services industry wide. Since Alloy has equity partners and lenders investing alongside, it must 'mark to market' to price architectural services; however, the consultancy and development market says nothing about the future value of an asset. Alloy is using design to create the additional tangible value and it leverages this economic value to realise other non-monetary goals.

Alloy's model is about leveraging the architectural skill set to create real-estate development opportunities. The partners use these skills to find better acquisitions, and the firm is more nimble than a traditional developer who has to rely on the expertise of an external architect. Unfortunately, it is not uncommon for a developer to take advantage of the marketplace and ask an architect to do concept work on spec

Alloy,
168 Plymouth Street,
Brooklyn, New York City,
due for completion 2020

The day after Alloy agreed to acquire 168 Plymouth
Street, plans were submitted to the New York
City Department of Buildings and the Landmarks
Preservation Commission with a proposal to add
two storeys to the existing historic structures,
saving six months.

in the hopes of being awarded the future commission, failing which the architect is not paid for this investment in time. This devalues the services of the architect and likely does not result in the best product for the developer. On the other hand, when Alloy spends the time internally to pursue an opportunity it is investing in the company and for the benefit of its future. The firm sees literally hundreds of potential projects and passes on most, but when the partners choose to spend time on an opportunity it is because they believe they can realise value that the rest of the market cannot. Alloy tends to be more successful when a site contains a degree of complexity and requires a clever solution and/or a unique vision.

Additionally, Alloy's model allows it to approach potential capital partners and lenders with a markedly more comprehensive investment memorandum, which results in certainty around what is being proposed, its cost and its anticipated future valuation. Ironically, by taking sole responsibility for the quality of the work and its outcomes, Alloy eliminates an extraordinary amount of risk.

Building Community

168 Plymouth Street (due for completion in 2020) is a 100,000-square-foot (9,000-square-metre) adaptive reuse of two historic warehouse buildings in Brooklyn. Built by Masury Paintworks in the late 19th century, the structures were combined into a single residential development containing 46 condominium apartments. Like many of Alloy's acquisitions, Alloy had attempted to purchase 168 Plymouth Street over a period of many years. When it came time to market the site officially, and the rest of the development community was trying to figure out what they would do, Alloy started schematic design. Alloy's planning was six months ahead of the competition. By the time of the bid deadline, Alloy was working from a full schematic design package, and knew exactly what the programme budget and strategy for development would be. When Alloy won the bid it immediately submitted plans to New York City's Department of Buildings and the Landmarks Preservation Commission the following day. During the contract period, Alloy invested and completed all of the pre-development work, and by the time Alloy closed on the asset the firm was mobilised for construction and was ready to start sales. Consequently, the loan term only needed to be 15 months instead of two and a half years, saving significant time and money.

The principals of Alloy are focused on alternative value propositions as a priority. In the case of 168 Plymouth Street, an entirely market-rate private development, Alloy is leveraging approximately US$130 million worth of condominium sales – and the ongoing revenue of building

In lieu of simply developing a building and taking the proceeds, Alloy is making a deliberate choice to invest locally and in the community

Alloy,
185 Plymouth Street,
Della Valle Residence,
Brooklyn, New York City,
2014

The principals of Alloy live in their own developments
to ensure the buildings are successfully managed over
the long term and to build community.

management to create potential community benefit. A unique governing structure is being tested whereby the building will have two governing boards. One board will manage the building and interests of the condominium in a traditional manner, and a separate, elective board will participate in administering a donor-advised fund that will be managed by the Brooklyn Community Foundation, the first and public foundation solely dedicated to Brooklyn's charitable community. The fund will be seeded through donations by Alloy as well as any annual building operations savings the residents choose to donate. The intent is to invest in the local community and the traditionally disenfranchised in Brooklyn at large. In lieu of simply developing a building and taking the proceeds, Alloy is making a deliberate choice to invest locally and in the community. The firm believes that a buyer who is purchasing a multimillion-dollar apartment in Brooklyn acknowledges and recognises that they are part of a broader community. Among other things, the fund may provide grants to support not-for-profits in the community that provide services to those who are food challenged, are homeless or need job training, and it could also support the arts or any other programmes as both the Brooklyn Community Foundation and the community of homeowners see fit. This has never been done before and it was quite difficult to initiate, but it is one of the many ways that Alloy seeks to leverage the opportunities from the tangible value of its work to generate future intangible value for the community.

Alloy,
One John Street,
Brooklyn, New York City,
2017

The programme for One John Street included 42 residential condominiums above and a donated annexe to the Brooklyn Children's Museum at ground level to expand the park into the building for all seasons. The design blurs the boundary of public and private space and acknowledges the privilege of building in a public park.

The Privilege of Public-Private Partnerships

Alloy was awarded One John Street, the last waterfront site in Brooklyn's DUMBO neighbourhood, through a public request for proposal (RFP) process in late 2013. The criterion for selection was a combination of both design excellence and economic certainty. Located at the north end of Brooklyn Bridge Park, One John Street is one of only two buildings in New York City situated entirely within a public park. Alloy served as the design architect, architect of record, developer (in collaboration with Monadnock) and real-estate broker.

The 130,000-square-foot (12,000-square-metre) building opened in 2017 and includes 42 apartments, the SPARK annexe for the Brooklyn Children's Museum, and retail space facing the waterfront. The long-term ground lease for One John Street finances ongoing maintenance and operations for the park over the next century. Through the donation of public programme, the design blurs the boundary of public and private space and acknowledges the privilege of building in public space.

The ground-floor space for the museum was donated to the park for US$1 along with the build-out of space and support for the operations of the early childhood education programme. This public space acknowledges the history of DUMBO and its transition from a thriving artist community to a vibrant mixed-use neighbourhood.

Alloy does not typically invest in advertising but it does use marketing resources to invest in the local community. As part of this effort, Alloy created the John Street Pasture (2014) as a public art project prior to building One John Street. Since the project location was inside a public park that was inaccessible during construction, Alloy decided to invert the relationship of park and site by building a park on its property in the interim. These efforts built awareness about where the project would be, and exposed Alloy's value set to the community. As a marketing tool it was memorable for potential buyers and located the future building but also became a piece of public art and a gesture towards the community.

By controlling the programme and finances of the project, Alloy was able to create the SPARK space for the Brooklyn Children's Museum, offering interior programme space for the park along with free after-school activity options for the local community.

Alloy,
80 Flatbush,
Brooklyn,
New York City,
due for completion 2022

80 Flatbush is a full-block mixed-use assemblage in downtown Brooklyn with over 1.1 million square feet (102,000 square metres) of space which includes the donation of two public schools, a cultural institution and over 200 units of affordable housing.

Rather than how much can we make, how much can we contribute?

Scaling to Change

Alloy's work addresses design problems by embracing the complexity that comes with making decisions that are simultaneously economic, political, legal and hopefully have a social component as well. This ability to solve problems simultaneously with a design solution is what makes working at Alloy so exciting.

Given Alloy's successful track record in generating tangible return on investment, the firm increasingly has the wherewithal to take on projects of expanding scale. The limitation on a firm's work really comes from the market's perception of its capacity, which for Alloy has changed dramatically over the last few years. Alloy wants to do more with each project that it develops, and its lenders and equity partners have increasingly given it the freedom to do so. But the intangible values generated by Alloy's projects are indicative of what it is focused on these days. Alloy's goal is to leverage scale and to answer the question: 'Rather than how much can we make, how much can we contribute?' ᴆ

Craig Curtis

Architecture at Scale

Reimagining One-Off Projects as Building Platforms

The building industry is fraught with delays, lack of coordination on site and budget overruns. **Craig Curtis**, Head of Architecture and Interior Design at off-site construction company Katerra, describes how his firm's fully integrated, reverse-engineered, prefabricated housing units mitigate this.

Katerra,
Workforce Housing –
Garden Building
Platform,
Seattle, Washington,
2019

The clean lines of Katerra's contemporary architecture allow for a limited palette of exterior finish materials that can be combined in various ways to yield variety. This platform was developed to respond to the need for workforce housing, those with an annual income of 80 to 120 per cent of Area Median Income (AMI).

The current global housing crisis has hit almost every city in the world, and the architecture, engineering and construction (AEC) industry needs to respond by providing scaleable resources to meet this demand. The traditional, industry-driven process of designing one-off multifamily homes that are then turned over to a construction manager at risk (CMAR) delivery method or general contractor to send out to bid, is cumbersome and inefficient. Pricing, quality, safety, collaboration and innovation all suffer. Architects have a unique role in designing more efficient processes and creating higher-quality designs that can be brought to market more expeditiously, at the same time driving down the cost of production.

Over the past decade, significant advancements in technology, specifically design software, have not only changed the way architects 'draw' projects, but also moulded the design process. Using new computational design software, architects can quickly evaluate thousands of design permutations graphically, without having to draw out each component to see how they fit together. Coordination between the various disciplines (architecture, electrical, structural, mechanical, security, plumbing and fire protection) is now made easier with building information modelling (BIM) software, which allows the whole team to work within one model. A single model allows for ease of clash detection and myriad other issues that can be flagged in the drawing phase and updated throughout the construction phase to address any real-time issues on site.

The Miller Hull Partnership,
Novotny Cabin,
Decatur Island, Washington,
1998

This cabin was fully documented by hand. Even though it is a small cabin, it only required eight sheets of drawings including electrical and structural. All materials were brought in by barge; construction lasted six months.

However, the use of this advanced technology often only results in the architect's compulsion to add more and more two-dimensional information to the set of drawings used for construction. Much of this information is superfluous and does nothing to significantly improve the way the building is assembled. Technology affords the industry a tremendous opportunity to improve design and construction for the future, but to capitalise on this potential requires a shift in mindset and understanding of how to perform the job of architect. Architects therefore need to move from a focus on one-off projects to creating building platforms that leverage technology to solve real, programmatic challenges and develop off-site manufacturing processes.

While other major industries have undergone radical modernisation, the AEC industry still relies on practices first introduced more than a hundred years ago. The causes of this stagnation and inefficiency are many. In 2016, 70 per cent of construction firms dedicated 1 per cent or less of their revenue to technology.[1] The industry is not even efficient in applying new technology. As Aaron Betsky has cited, technology in the built environment has been used to further our realm of 'possible' designs as opposed to making them more efficient or technologically sound: 'The big change came with the advent of computer modeling and drawing, which let architects draw forms that they could only imagine before … justification to use this new technology was that this was a more organic way of building, one that distributed forces and material in a more efficient manner.'[2]

Embracing Technology
The design and construction industry has seen an annual productivity increase of only 1 per cent since the Second World War, while productivity in other sectors such as agriculture, manufacturing and retail has soared.[3] Many other industries, particularly product-based and manufacturing, are so far ahead that it is embarrassing. The lack of investment in technology is partially to blame; however, while this is an issue, it is also an opportunity to leverage the learning curves of other industries that have already capitalised on it. Much knowledge can be gained by looking at how product-based industries have advanced with innovations such as Tesla's automobile factories, Foxconn's assembly lines and Amazon's distribution capabilities. There are common lessons that can be applied to the design and construction of buildings.

The global urban population is growing in leaps and bounds, yet the affordability gap continues to widen. Though this is not a new issue, it is becoming more pressing by the day. To understand how to balance value and speed without compromising design and aesthetics, architects might look to the past. In 1936, Frank Lloyd Wright designed the Usonian House as a response to the need for a simple, stylish, American middle-class home at a moderate cost. A concept rather than a specific structure, it resulted in more than 60 iterations built throughout the US, including a planned community in Pleasantville, New York. 'Style *is* important,' wrote Wright. '*A* style is not.'[4] 'It is not only necessary to get rid of all unnecessary complications in construction,' he continued, 'it is necessary to consolidate and simplify the three appurtenance systems – heating, lighting, and sanitation.'[5]

The Miller Hull
Partnership,
Island House,
Bainbridge Island,
Washington,
2004

The house was designed using
AutoCAD with a drawing set of
over 200 sheets. The full team
worked together for more than
five years to complete the project,
from design through construction.

Wright coined the term 'Usonian Automatic' to describe these designs: 'To build a low-cost house you must eliminate, so far as possible, the use of skilled labor … now so expensive.'[6] His beautifully designed and affordable homes were laid out on a grid to standardise construction and make them easier to build and replicate. Materials were simple – stone, concrete, wood and brick – and were left unpainted to express their texture and materiality. Katerra is embracing technology by applying Wright's vision of standardisation and ease of construction processes in three important ways: vertical integration, productised design and off-site manufacturing.

Vertical Integration

Construction is one of the most inefficient and fragmented industries in the world. Katerra leverages the supply chain for building into one company, enabling it to drive efficiency in the entire design and build process by removing layers of markup, correspondence and handoffs, and creating full end-to-end transparency with total control over the areas of risk such as schedule, availability, safety, and quality and cost control. The firm's vertical integration affords new considerations and efficiencies in the design process. Its in-house line of products can be capitalised upon to drive down the overall cost of the project, as opposed to looking at one piece or part at a time. Its catalogue of beautiful, replicable items can be used throughout projects, with clear specifications built into the plans, in contrast to designing for one-off configurations that waste materials and time and require special installation in the field.

Frank Lloyd Wright,
Usonian House,
Lakeland, Florida,
1939

The Usonian House was designed as a kit
of parts using the same grid system built
in at least 60 locations across the US. Each
is unique in appearance based on the
individuals' selections.

KEY ASSEMBLIES

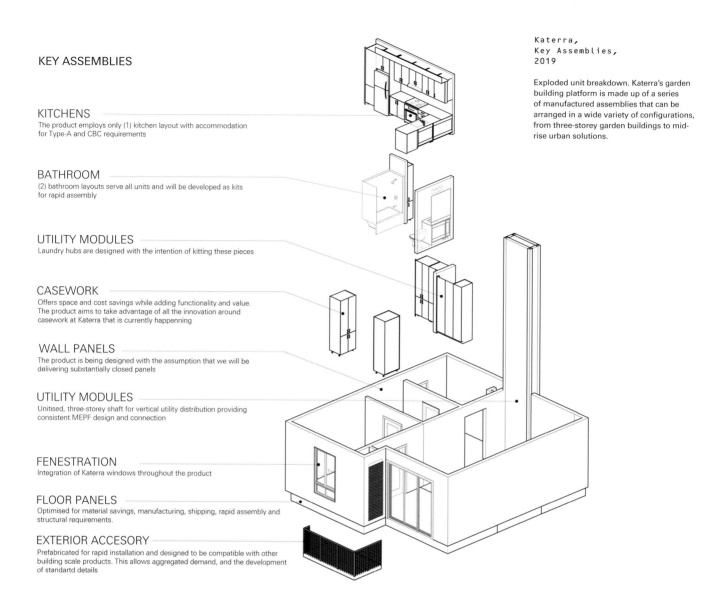

Exploded unit breakdown. Katerra's garden building platform is made up of a series of manufactured assemblies that can be arranged in a wide variety of configurations, from three-storey garden buildings to mid-rise urban solutions.

KITCHENS
The product employs only (1) kitchen layout with accommodation for Type-A and CBC requirements

BATHROOM
(2) bathroom layouts serve all units and will be developed as kits for rapid assembly

UTILITY MODULES
Laundry hubs are designed with the intention of kitting these pieces

CASEWORK
Offers space and cost savings while adding functionality and value. The product aims to take advantage of all the innovation around casework at Katerra that is currently happenning

WALL PANELS
The product is being designed with the assumption that we will be delivering substantially closed panels

UTILITY MODULES
Unitised, three-storey shaft for vertical utility distribution providing consistent MEPF design and connection

FENESTRATION
Integration of Katerra windows throughout the product

FLOOR PANELS
Optimised for material savings, manufacturing, shipping, rapid assembly and structural requirements.

EXTERIOR ACCESORY
Prefabricated for rapid installation and designed to be compatible with other building scale products. This allows aggregated demand, and the development of standartd details

Katerra,
Market-Rate Housing -
Garden Building Platform,
Seattle, Washington,
2019

Katerra's catalogue of interior products and finishes has been carefully curated to create a timeless design aesthetic.

Productised Design

Most building projects finish over budget and behind schedule. It is shocking that this is a recognised and acceptable fact in the industry; no other industry would be so accepting of it. A significant contributing factor here starts with design; the majority of buildings are one-offs requiring architects to redraw every aspect each time, where the many disparate elements, various materials and labour needs lead to high levels of unpredictability. Designers do not have to work in this vacuum; they can instead embrace approaches perfected by other industries by thinking of buildings as 'products' and reimagining one-off projects as building platforms.

To establish smarter methods of designing a building's structure and systems, Katerra reverse-engineered a full building, breaking it down into component parts. The result is a building platform, a highly coordinated, fully optimised solution to garden-style, workforce and market-rate walk-up residential housing. A 12-unit plan, the Market-Rate Housing comprises one studio, five one-bedrooms, four two-bedrooms, and two three-bedrooms that can be arranged into various combinations to support a variety of unit mixes based on client and site needs. These efficient and easily repeatable units are designed around a central core, or 'utility spine', that services the three-storey vertical utility shafts that intersect it. The Workforce Housing model includes only three building configurations and three unit types, and is further optimised to meet the cost targets for this type of housing.

The platform uses as few unique parts as possible by adopting a productised component approach. Each building type is broken down into manufactured assemblies, for example bathroom and kitchen kits, wall and panels loaded with building services, and casework, while still being flexible enough in design to meet customers' individual needs. The assemblies and products are shared across the platform, responding to market demands and cost targets while allowing for unique design elements to be added as necessary. Similar platforms are being developed by Katerra to serve other markets including senior, student housing and single-family housing and commercial office space.

Katerra advanced manufacturing facility,
Phoenix, Arizona,
2019

The firm's factories utilise automated equipment and processes to reduce labour costs and increase accuracy and efficiency.

Katerra's first cross-laminated timber (CLT) commercial office building is designed to be net zero energy. This is also the first building based on Katerra's Commercial Office Building Platform, utilising a standard kit of parts based on the manufacturing capabilities of Katerra's CLT factory.

Detailed and accurate designs include preloading every wall panel with the necessary plumbing and electrical services

The firm's off-site manufacturing capabilities expand the true benefit of productised design, with as much of the construction work as possible moved from the field to the factory to enable greater quality control, safety and speed. Detailed and accurate designs include preloading every wall panel with the necessary plumbing and electrical services in Katerra's wall-integrated mechanical system. At the same time, the firm is also embracing new technologies when it comes to materials, specifically cross-laminated timber (CLT). It recently opened its first CLT factory, which adopts cutting-edge technology to press CLT panels up to 12 x 60 feet (4 x 18 metres)

Integrated Design

Architects working on a multifamily building with a set of repeatable units usually begin the schematic design process by placing blocks that represent the units over a site plan as a way of developing an initial parti. As the design develops, there is a play between these fixed components and the flexible parts of the building in response to site and programmatic considerations, the resolution of which is expressed in the finished design. In the Katerra model, the building blocks are actually fully designed components, completed to a level of detail typically reserved for shop drawings prepared by subcontractors and fabricators, with all building systems fully integrated. This means that once the schematic design is complete, the architects spend the balance of the project taking the unique aspects such as the building envelope and common areas to component-design level, ready to be sent to the factory floor.

The level of precision and specificity required in manufacturing building products, and in designing a scaleable system that responds to such a broad set of needs, is considerably higher than that for traditional stick-building or one-off projects. Balancing the efficiencies of off-site manufacturing with the realities of customer needs and a commitment to design quality is critical if we are to produce the high standard and quantity of housing solutions necessary to meet global need. Critics claim that prefabricated buildings curtail creativity and aesthetic freedom, but constraint-driven design prioritises function over form, and is therefore the truest expression of good design.

If we are to solve some of the most challenging social crises facing humanity today, such as the massive shortage of workforce housing, we must make dramatic changes to the process. Integrated project delivery needs to take advantage of technology in new ways and go well beyond design and engineering to include off-site manufacturing, materials sourcing and streamlined field assembly. Such a new approach to delivering buildings is reliant on architects developing the building platforms to define this process, finally allowing the productivity gains that until now have eluded our industry. ∆

Notes
1. JBKnowledge, *The 5th Annual Construction Technology Report*, 2016: https://jbknowledge.com/wp-content/uploads/2017/09/2016_JBKnowledge_Construction_Technology_Report.pdf.
2. Aaron Betsky, 'Robotic Innovation', *ARCHITECT*, 1 February 2019: www.architectmagazine.com/design/robotic-innovation_o.
3. Filipe Barbosa *et al, Reinventing Construction: A Route to Higher Productivity*, McKinsey Global Institute, February 2017, p 23: www.mckinsey.com/~/media/McKinsey/Industries/Capital%20Projects%20and%20Infrastructure/Our%20Insights/Reinventing%20construction%20through%20a%20productivity%20revolution/MGI-Reinventing-construction-A-route-to-higher-productivity-Full-report.ashx.
4. Frank Lloyd Wright, *Frank Lloyd Wright: An Autobiography*, Pomegranate Communications (Petaluma, CA), 2005, p 490.
5. *Ibid*.
6. Frank Lloyd Wright and Bruce Brooks Pfeiffer, *The Essential Frank Lloyd Wright: Critical Writings on Architecture,* Princeton University Press (Princeton, NJ), 2008, p 16.

AUTOMA
AND MA
LEARNI
IN
A NEW AGENDA FOR
ARCHIT

TION
CHINE
NG

Sandeep Ahuja and **Patrick Chopson**

PERFORMANCE-DRIVEN DESIGN

ECTURE

In the modern context it is important to be able to analyse building performance data at the initial stages of the design. This allows spaces to be optimised environmentally with fewer cost implications. **Sandeep Ahuja and Patrick Chopson**, founders of the Atlanta, Georgia firm Pattern r+d, have developed cove.tool software for the purpose.

The mounting effects of climate change on the environment are a powerful catalyst to articulate a new vision for architecture. If the profession is to become fact- and data-driven and responsible to the planet, alternatives to traditional practice must be found to foster innovation. Venture capital investment is lowering the barriers to entry for new types of startups that are building capabilities enabling the future of practice. Cove.tool is one such venture that has taken a non-traditional approach to the delivery of building energy analysis into the market.

During previous experience working in a large multinational architecture firm performing analysis on a wide range of high-profile projects, it became clear that architectural practices are unable to afford simulation on most projects.[1] Continuous simulation capabilities are needed during design iteration, since testing only a few options is like trying to navigate in the wilderness while infrequently checking a compass. However, relying on either in-house specialist teams or external consultants is too expensive for routine schematic phase analysis. An often-proposed alternative is to train architects to run their own simulations, but typical analysis packages are developed by researchers for use by specialists with years of experience, and require extensive knowledge of inputs and underlying science. Training all staff to use them would be cost prohibitive, and anyway the overheads and additional work would prevent them from running the necessary iterations. The best way to integrate rational decision-making into this aspect of design is to give architects tools to quickly and easily run models for themselves without needing specialised knowledge. The cost of human labour is the roadblock to data-driven design in traditional practice, not a lack of desire.

cove.tool,
Massing studies for
Campus Life Center,
Emory University,
Atlanta, Georgia,
2018

The impact of building massing on energy performance. Fast, accurate simulation makes evaluation of alternatives significantly easier for design decision making. Without the use of automation, a simple, iterative design study like this would take a skilled energy modeller 20 to 30 hours.

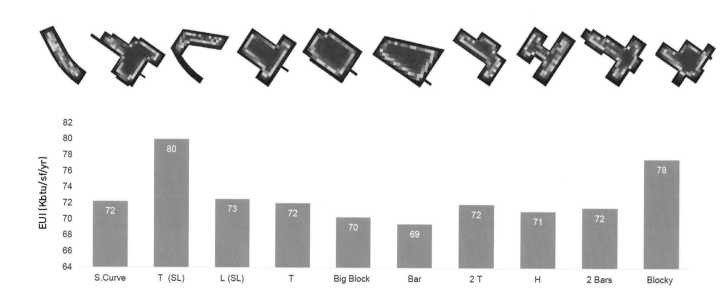

The sustainability consulting practice Pattern r+d was launched in 2015 to respond to the challenges outlined above. While acquiring clients and consulting on projects, the firm immediately began automating each step of the consulting process, with the ultimate goal of eliminating the need for its services.

The team uncovered large gaps in the data flows between professions and at different stages of the design process. The engineers struggled to access the building geometry and run enough simulations for the architect. Contractors were unable to obtain pricing in the early stages or evaluate alternatives based on performance. Frustrated owners could not evaluate whether design proposals were either high performance or cost effective. At the centre of it all, architects tried their best to manage, but were ultimately overwhelmed by the volume of data. Each gap in the decision-making process added time and cost. Through this experience, Pattern r+d realised that in order to be effective, automation needs to be paired with a shared workspace.

In the process of automating workflows, it became clear that simulation tools often pursue meaningless accuracy improvements instead of speed and usability. All simulations are simplifications of reality and must produce repeatable, consistent guidance from the available information. Making too many detailed assumptions before the problem is well defined introduces uncertainty into the simulation. During the early design phase, the fewer assumptions entered into the model the more likely it is that the result will point the designer in the right direction. Along with fitting the complexity of the simulation to the decision to be made, speed is vital. If a result is 1 per cent more accurate but arrives a week later, it is useless. Low-resolution yet accurate simulations remove uncertainty and run faster than detailed models, making them more successful at guiding decision-making. Because the information to define additional parameters becomes more detailed as the project progresses, the software development of a large unified tool can proceed from low resolution to detailed compliance modelling. A philosophy of developing software from low- to high-resolution simulation is critical to bringing data-driven design to the profession.

Decision-making time and accuracy became a guiding principle for Pattern r+d's automation strategy. Instead of adopting detailed but computationally heavy simulation engines like EnergyPlus,[2] the firm uses an ultra-fast simulation method called ISO 13790.[3] Calibrating this engine with the engineer's modelling tools aligns all those involved around common benchmarking targets.

cove.tool,
Revit plugin interface,
2019

The plugin enables users to rapidly send key information from their BIM model for automated analysis. Data transfer is typically the greatest impediment to implementation, hence the decision to allow the importing of open geometry.

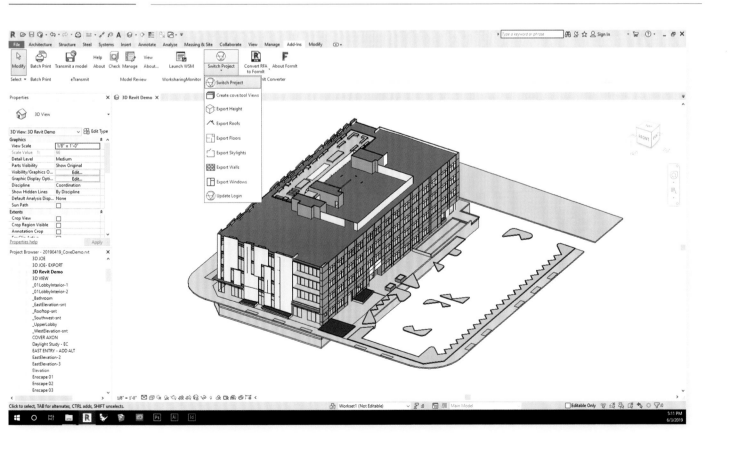

UNIFIED MACHINE LEARNING

Architects make hundreds of design decisions each week and coordinate a web of multi-objective problems. Automating tasks as individual scripts is manageable only as long as the number of tasks remains small, as every design problem involves conflicting needs. Selecting a window product involves balancing HVAC systems, aesthetics, energy, daylight, glare, thermal comfort and cost. Faced with an explosion of data and options, many designers resign themselves to using the same glass as on their previous project or are swayed by the most recent salesperson's visit. Pattern r+d thus identified the need for a unified machine learning software for managing tradeoffs among the various scripts in the form of a simplified graphical user interface. Building upon decades of research at the Georgia Institute of Technology, the team began hacking together the first version of the cove.tool (cost versus energy) software platform.

Development of the tool was initially funded through the consulting business. With a strong focus on usability, the team began shaping the software into a robust user-friendly product. Even with limited features, it could be beta tested in the consulting practice. However, it soon became clear that venture capital would be necessary to launch a product that could scale. Armed with a working prototype, the cove.tool team entered a startup competition for funding, and won.

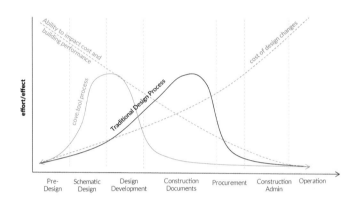

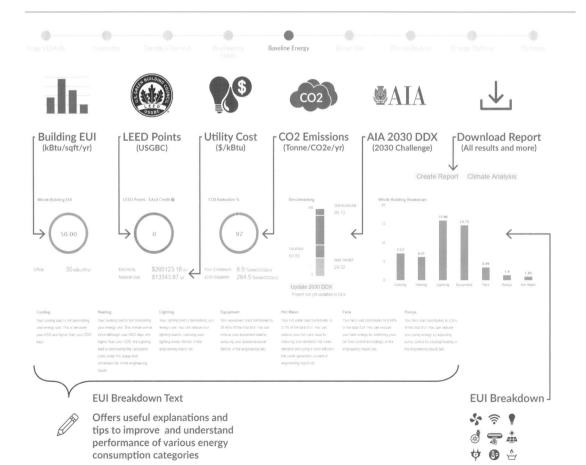

EUI Breakdown Text

Offers useful explanations and tips to improve and understand performance of various energy consumption categories

EUI Breakdown

cove.tool,
MacLeamy's Curve,
2019

MacLeamy's Curve highlights that current practice pushes performance analysis to later in the design phase when it is least economical to make any design changes. Cove.tool brings this analysis forward, to the earlier part of the design process when the opportunity to impact cost and performance is highest.

cove.tool,
Baseline energy results,
2019

Snapshot from cove.tool showcasing a variety of building performance results that design teams can use to better inform their building process. Similar software tools, for building performance and other data-driven decisions, are starting to penetrate the industry. This study took Pattern r+d over 40 hours to prepare as part of their consulting practice. In cove.tool the analysis took just 10 minutes.

Duda|Paine Architects,
Campus Life Center,
Emory University,
Atlanta, Georgia,
2019

opposite: The architects worked in close collaboration with engineers IMEG and the university's capital planning and design group on the data-driven decision making for this high-performance centre. Using cove.tool, the design team was able to analyse over 3,000 design alternatives and select the optimal solution.

Cove.tool,
Optimisation interface,
2019

Parallel coordinates plots are
useful for linking together
bundles of decisions and their
impacts. Multi-objective cost-
versus-energy optimisation
allows users to select the option
that is optimal not just for
performance, but cost too.

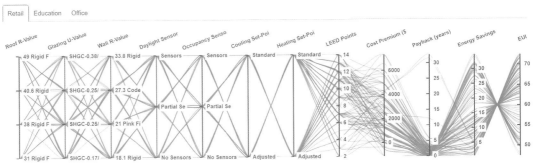

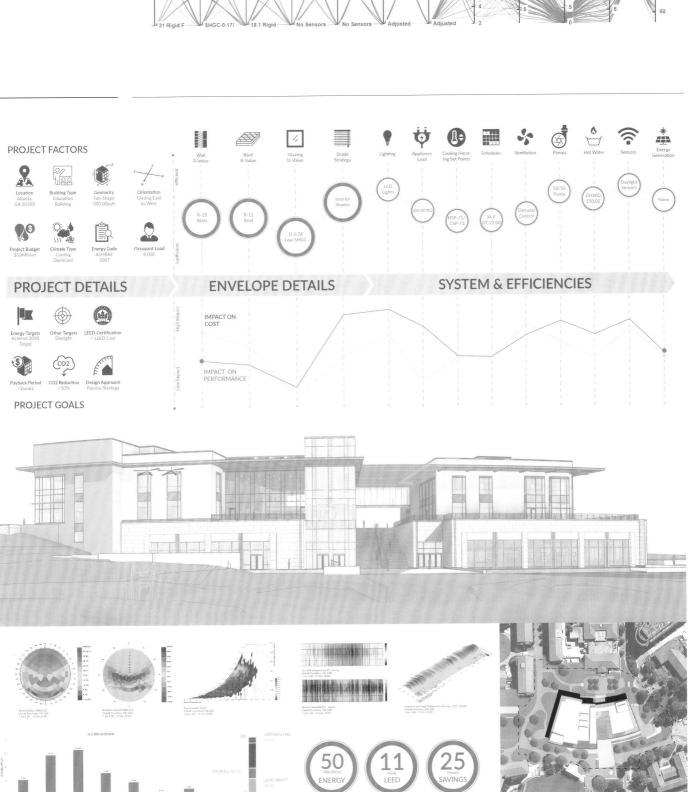

Data-driven, parametric and responsible,
it is a paradigm for a modern architecture
that reflects the needs and aspirations
of the 21st century

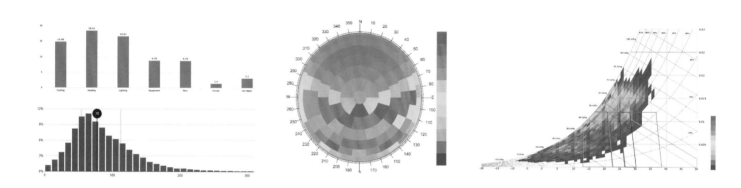

This allowed cove.tool to scale up, making the software accessible to hundreds of firms. By enabling smarter, more accurate models to be built and tested quickly, a range of building alternatives can be explored and the best one identified. Cost is a motivating factor for most projects. The platform also simplifies the use of machine learning by giving algorithms a common scoring mechanism for each design alternative. Thousands of alternatives can be compared in a few seconds, allowing optimisation of cost-versus-energy tradeoffs. With a database of cost values from manufacturers integrated into this optimisation cycle, users can typically find systems that cost 2 to 3 per cent less while simultaneously being 40 per cent more efficient.

It was a conscious decision to address energy analysis first, since changing energy codes force architects to pursue aggressive targets. Additional scripts for analysing daylight, glare, thermal comfort and water usage, developed for previous consulting projects, are now rapidly being incorporated within the cove.tool platform. Each of these metrics can be linked back to the costing model and incrementally managed by the machine-learning approach. The ultimate goal is to incorporate every data point crucial in the design process and automate all the tedious work for generating and managing this data.

Changing a profession requires collective responsibility and collective empowerment. With buildings contributing 40 per cent of carbon emissions, architects need to find new ways to enable them to make better environmental performance decisions. Machine learning can be a critical part of this future. By managing the complex data flows between different analyses, consultants, contractors and owners, machine-learning software returns the decision-making power to the architect. Data-driven, parametric and responsible, it is a paradigm for a modern architecture that reflects the needs and aspirations of the 21st century. ⌀

NOTES
1. American Institute of Architects (AIA), '2030 By the Numbers: The 2018 summary of the AIA 2020 Commitment', September 2019: http://content.aia.org/sites/default/files/2019-08/AIA_2030_ByTheNumbers_2018.pdf.
2. Drury B Crawley *et al*, 'EnergyPlus: Energy Simulation Program', *ASHRAE Journal*, 42 (4), April 2000, pp 49–56.
3. ISO 13790: Thermal Performance of Buildings – Calculation of Energy Use for Space Heating and Cooling, 2003–08. Found at: www.iso.org/standard/41974.html.

Cooper Carry Architects,
Campus Center,
Georgia Institute
of Technology,
Atlanta, Georgia,
2020

The architects worked in close collaboration with engineers Newcomb & Boyd and the Georgia Institute of Technology capital planning and design group on the data-driven decision making for the high-performance centre. Cove. tool was used for the performance analysis to showcase optimal use of every construction dollar to reduce energy use intensity (EUI).

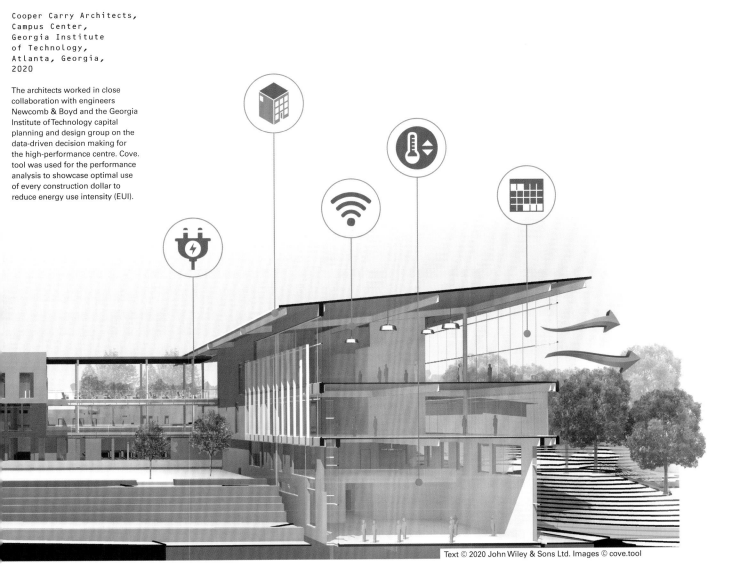

**Jesse Louis-Rosenberg and
Jessica Rosenkrantz**

ANTI-ENTRE

Nervous System,
Infinite Galaxy Puzzle,
2016

A new type of jigsaw puzzle based on
the Klein bottle that tiles continuously.
It has no fixed shape, no starting point
and no edges, and can be assembled
in thousands of different ways.

PRENEURS

USING
COMPUTATION
TO UNSCALE
PRODUCTION

Being multidisciplinary, digitally adept and small is the key to success of **Jesse Louis-Rosenberg and Jessica Rosenkrantz**'s generative design studio Nervous System in upstate New York that works at the intersection of science, art and technology. Their projects are inspired by natural phenomena and at once they are biological researchers, artists and coders. This synthesis of expertise and practice creates beautiful and thoughtful objects.

In business, technology is seen as a driver for change, by making things bigger, faster and more automated. However, it can also be leveraged to make products and businesses more personal, empowering and democratic. Rather than scaling up to bigger and better, how can computation be used in design to unscale? At Nervous System we explore how new technologies in manufacturing and computation enable innovative design at a human scale.

Nervous System is a design studio that specialises in computation and digital fabrication. Everything we design is created by software that we write, often inspired by natural phenomena like veins of leaves or the growth of coral. Instead of creating static designs, we create dynamic systems. Instead of drawing structures, we are interested in growing them. These generated designs are digitally fabricated using various computer-controlled manufacturing tools: 3D printing, laser cutting, CNC routing, photochemical etching. Using these techniques, we make everything from jewellery and jigsaw puzzles to facades and engineered human tissues.

The studio defies categorisation. We are designers that have the singular focus and vision normally ascribed to artists. We are artists that make affordable, everyday objects. We are jewellers who work more with code than a torch. We are software developers who manufacture and sell physical things. We are a gift stop that does advanced bioengineering research. We are a non-start startup that has forgone investment and exponential growth in favour of a simple steady existence as a small business.

Jessica Rosenkrantz assembling
Dendrite Collection brooches
at her desk,
Harvard University Graduate
School of Design (GSD),
Cambridge, Massachusetts,
2007

Nervous System began in 2007 when Jesse and Jessica were studying at the Harvard Graduate School of Design (GSD) and Massachusetts Institute of Technology (MIT). Their first products were made in the digital fabrication lab at Harvard and sold on Etsy.

Nervous System,
Coral necklaces,
2007

opposite: The first series of one-of-a-kind jewellery from Nervous System, part of the Dendrite Collection. To date, over 2,500 unique necklaces have been produced and sold.

Beginnings

In many ways this whole endeavour was an accident. We started Nervous System in 2007 when we were both still in school. Jesse was a disaffected math major that had dabbled in artificial intelligence and quickly came to the conclusion that it had nothing to do with intelligence at all. Jessica was a biology major turned architect whose obsession with natural forms and hexagons was not much appreciated by her instructors. In the early 2000s, computation in architecture was still a fringe and often-maligned idea. In fact, as an undergrad, Jessica's architecture classes at MIT still required drawing everything by hand. Needless to say, our experiments in design and computation did not feel like they had a home.

One day, while assembling an architectural model made of laser-cut chipboard, a classmate walked by and asked Jessica if the piece was a bracelet. 'No, that's my building,' she replied. But as she sat at her desk, struggling with model pieces strewn every which way, she thought it would actually make a pretty cool bracelet. We laser-cut a couple of them late at night in the Harvard basement, posted them on Flickr and Etsy, and sold one the very next day. This validation helped us realise that we could pursue these topics – complex systems, the formation of natural structures, digital fabrication and design – on our own terms. If you can reach people directly and find those who appreciate your work, it does not matter what major institutions say.

Despite this coincidental occurrence, Nervous System began with a specific vision in mind. We were inspired by the idea of the Fab Lab as a place where anyone could make anything. There was a promise that digital fabrication could do to objects what the Internet did with ideas and expression. Computation offered new ways to engage with design; people talked about these ideas, but did not execute them. We wanted these things not to be limited to academia or $10,000 teapots. This was not some theoretical idea, but something that could be done right now. We launched Nervous System with two jewellery collections, Dendrite and Radiolaria. Each came with an accompanying app, a software system where anyone could design their own piece with the same algorithms we used. We made one-of-a-kind, generatively designed and customised products that sold for between $15 and $75.

In some ways, displacing the impersonal and wasteful model of mass production with bespoke mass customisation mediated by computation may seem to be a disruptive agenda. It is a rallying cry that another way is possible. However, contemporary disruption has taken on another connotation. When we think about the Ubers of the world, the disruption they have brought is not so much a new way of doing things, but a technologically mediated market takeover. Despite the Internet's initial promise to bring decentralisation and empower the many over the few, technology's ability to scale has led to increasing centralisation of many industries. What we are looking for at Nervous System is not simply ways to supplant existing structures, but ways that technology can enrich our current experience.

Generative Jigsaw Puzzles: Computation + Craft

When we began making laser-cut jigsaw puzzles in 2012, our intention was not to disrupt the jigsaw-puzzle market. In fact, it was almost the opposite. Today, jigsaw puzzles are synonymous with cardboard toys where images are cut into simple, repetitive interlocking shapes. However, they were originally handcrafted from wood and have a rich history dating back to the 18th century. Technological innovation precipitated this new art form with the invention of the mechanical scroll saw. Puzzle makers developed their own styles with beautifully intricate pieces that were cut entirely freehand. Each puzzle was therefore one of a kind and often included thematic figural pieces in recognisable shapes like dancers or ships that matched their accompanying image. This art largely died out with the advent of mass production, which disrupted the wooden-puzzle industry by supplying a cheaper alternative in the form of die-cut cardboard.

Our aim is to use technology not to copy or automate traditional wooden puzzles, but to revive their spirit and artistry for a new age. Laser cutting enables even more intricate and precise cutting of wood. What possibilities does this technological innovation open up for jigsaw puzzles?

By combining laser cutting and computational design, we grow puzzles where every piece is unique and each image is different. The cuts are based on a simulation of dendritic solidification. This is a crystal growth process that occurs in supercooled fluids where intricate branches form as the liquid freezes. To make this work as a puzzle, the binary relationship of liquid and solid needs to be broken. Each puzzle piece is its own phase of matter, simultaneously growing into each other. The result is that just like hand-cut puzzles, each one has a different set of pieces. To date, we have manufactured and sold over 6,000 unique puzzles.

We wanted to go further and ask what we might do with computational design and fabrication to challenge what a puzzle is. What if a puzzle had no edge? People normally start a puzzle from its edge as the straight pieces are easily recognisable. By taking the edge away, we subvert the typical puzzle strategy and force people to reconsider how they do it. But what does making an edgeless puzzle mean? A puzzle that has no edge is a puzzle that tiles. Pieces from one side connect to the other, meaning the puzzle has no fixed shape and can be assembled in thousands of different ways. To borrow from mathematics, a tiling puzzle has the topology of a torus. Taking the idea of an edgeless puzzle further, we can think of other topological spaces. A Klein bottle is similar to a torus, except the left side connects to the right with a flip. This is what makes a Klein bottle non-orientable. It has no inside or outside. If you try to travel along the outside surface, you end up inside and vice versa. If you make a puzzle using this same idea, it is non-orientable. It has no bottom or top side. Pieces from the left side connect to the right, but only after flipping over. Our Infinite Galaxy Puzzle (2016) combines the topology of a Klein bottle with an image from the Hubble Telescope of the Milky Way. The result is a never-ending, double-sided puzzle where each time you assemble it, you see a different part of the galaxy.

Nervous System,
Geode Puzzle,
2017

A series of one-of-a-kind puzzles inspired by the form of banded agate. Each puzzle has a different shape, image and cut.

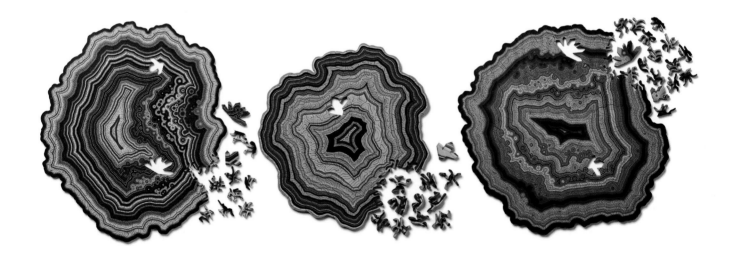

People normally start a puzzle from its edge as the straight pieces are easily recognisable. By taking the edge away, we subvert the typical puzzle strategy and force people to reconsider how they do it

Kinematics Dress: Computation + Customisation

Nervous System probes the ways in which technology can change how we design. Not merely using technology to automate; nor using it solely to explore new aesthetic effects, but examining the possibilities of new technology for making design more accessible. Instead of designing products, we design processes. These are encoded as open-ended software that consumers can engage with to create their own customised designs. The tools are not general CAD software, but specific design experiences. They are a product that is also a process.

The Kinematics Dress project (2013–18) looks at how this approach can change the way we design clothing. 3D printers primarily print hard material and the flexible materials are not robust enough for end use. To create a 3D-printable fabric, we looked at mechanisms that allow for motion. By connecting many triangular units with hinges, we get something that approaches cloth. These hinged, tessellated constructions are an interesting hybrid between soft and hard materials. Each element is rigid, but in aggregate they flow fluidly. As we printed small samples, we dreamt of expanding beyond the confines of the print bed to make larger-scale constructions. How would a long dress made from this hard/soft material feel? How would it flow and move?

The digital fabrication of large objects usually requires breaking them down into small unique pieces that have to be organised and assembled into the final object by hand – a task often more difficult and time-consuming than any other part of the project, where computation makes life more difficult, not easier. But what if they could be printed all in one piece? The Kinematics Dress takes advantage of the fact that the structures we are making are flexible. By computationally bending and folding them, we calculate a smaller configuration in which they can be fabricated. A large complex design is then printed in a compressed configuration that unfolds from the printer into its intended shape. This has changed the way we think about designing clothing. Bodies are three-dimensional, but clothing design normally happens in flat patterns and flat material. By designing directly on 3D scans of the body, we make truly custom-fit garments where nothing has to be cut, sewn or assembled.

The Kinematics Cloth website opens up this process to non-designers, allowing anyone to create their own 3D-printable clothes. Customers start with a 3D scan or measurements to input their body shape. They can sculpt the silhouette of their garment and even design the structure of the fabric itself. By painting on density, porosity and shape, the user can specify the units that make up the garment, creating a variable textile, the different areas of which have different structural properties

Nervous System,
Kinematics Cloth app,
2014

The app provides an intuitive painting interface where anyone can design their own garment as well as save, share and remix others.

Nervous System,
Kinematics Dress #6,
2015

Made of thousands of unique components, the custom-fit garment requires no assembly. Though each component is rigid, in aggregate they flow and move with the body.

controlled by the user, unlike most textiles which are uniform except for colour. After the design is complete, we use a rigid body physics solver to heuristically fold the design into a shape that fits inside the print volume.

The project highlights how computation can create new workflows to challenge mass manufacturing. It proposes a way to make fully customised garments that are self-designed by consumers by combining data, co-creation software, simulation and digital manufacturing.

Bio-printing Organs: Computation + Interdisciplinarity

Designing systems can not only change the relationship of the designer to the consumer, but also enable new opportunities for design intervention. Since 2016 we have been collaborating with a bioengineering lab at Rice University in Houston, Texas, which is developing methods to 3D-print human tissue. What quickly became clear as we began working together is that there is no 3D design tool for biological structures. Functional tissues require structures with complexity that rival what we see in organisms, which adapt to different constraints and conditions. Effective research into blending biology, engineering and 3D modelling needs new types of tools. Many of the tools and techniques that have been developed to generate complex forms in computational design and architecture can inform the development of tools for bioengineering.

Designing systems can not only change the relationship of the designer to the consumer, but also enable new opportunities for design intervention

Nervous System
and the Miller Lab,
Lung Mimetic
Architecture,
Rice University,
Houston, Texas,
2019

left: The alveoli-like structure was printed in human stem cells using a new bioprinting method called SLATE that was developed at the Miller Lab and perfused with red blood cells.

below: Alveoli units are joined together with three intertwining networks to allow for blood and air circulation. The networks can be grown inside an arbitrary volume.

The Miller Lab at Rice is developing a new method called SLATE that enables the fabrication of intricate living structures from cells suspended in hydrogel by stereolithography. Rather than printing a scaffold that is later impregnated with living material, the cells are printed directly in place. This allows for the creation of more complex structures than were previously possible. One of the difficulties in 3D-printing tissue is how to keep the cells alive afterwards. For small or thin tissues, nutrients and oxygen can be supplied simply by diffusion. However, larger, more complex tissues require vascular structures such as blood vessel networks to support them. How do we design such structures?

Nervous System is collaborating with the Miller Lab to develop a suite of tools for computational tissue engineering. The goal is to create an open-source software that researchers and practitioners could use to generate biological structures. Specifically, we are creating a system to produce the intricate vascular networks needed to support 3D-printed tissues. The software generates not just blood vessel networks, but also interpenetrating networks like the intertwining blood and air vessels seen in our lungs. Instead of needing to painstakingly 3D-model the blood vessel networks (which may be different for each patient), the generative software allows us to create networks customised to design constraints such as flow, direction and shape.

We have begun by developing a generative lung-mimetic architecture based on an alveolar sac, the tiny respiring units that make up the lungs. The geometry is a grape-like air cavity ensheathed by cellular capillary-like veins that are oriented to the direction of flow using an anisotropic, centroidal voronoi structure. While only one of these alveoli-esque structures can currently be printed, they are designed to connect to a hierarchical lung-like airway intertwined with two blood vessel networks: one to bring deoxygenated blood and another to take the oxygen-rich blood away. Given a volume shape and an air inlet location, the system packs the volume with alveoli units and connects them together with three networks: air, blood-in and blood-out. The proof of concept was printed in living cells and artificially respirated. While still an order of magnitude larger than real alveoli, this represents a leap forward in the complexity of engineered tissue.

Computation + Unscaling

Nervous System is a small, self-funded, research-focused design studio that poses an alternative to startups and large institutions. Despite its small scale, the studio has had a significant influence on contemporary design practice, acting as a case study for the real-life implementation of mass customisation, simulation and 3D printing. Perhaps its most 'disruptive' aspect is not what we design or the way we design, but how we have shown that a studio does not need massive growth to have global impact. We believe that technology enables small-scale production and the democratisation of design. This does not mean creating the Google of mass customisation, but that thousands of small design firms can thrive by exploring their own niches. ᴆ

Text © 2020 John Wiley & Sons Ltd. Images: pp 112–16, 117(l),
118–19(b) © Nervous System; p 117(r) © 2015 Steve Marsel
Studio stevemarselstudio.com; p 118–19(t) © Jordan S Miller

Architects = Innovators (sometimes) Innovators ≠ Entrepreneurs (most of the time)

Greg Lynn, founder-owner of Greg Lynn FORM and currently a professor at the University of Applied Arts Vienna and at the University of California Los Angeles (UCLA), has been at the forefront of the architectural digital revolution since the early 1990s. Here he explains why historically architects are not entrepreneurs, and implores them to think outside the box and innovate by stealing back and owning the digitised means of production for architecture, infrastructure and products.

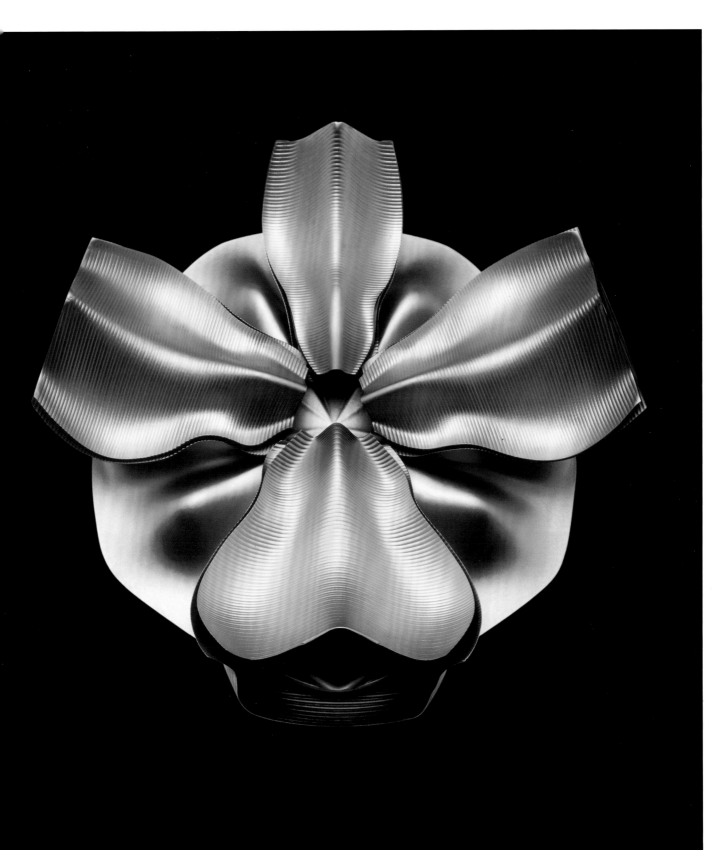

Greg Lynn FORM,
Alessi Tea and Coffee Tower,
2003

Made from super-formed titanium with inner flasks and
temperature-isolated outer shells for gripping, the tea
and coffee service sits on a reversible base so can be
carried and displayed upright or lying down.

Innovation starts with a new problem, not a new answer. Entrepreneurship follows innovation with the right answer, at the right time, for the right price. There is no intrinsic relationship between innovation and entrepreneurship as a skill set or even demeanour. If an innovator is also an entrepreneur, it is most likely due to a lack of patience. An entrepreneur's skill is to understand culture in order to identify market opportunity, calibrate the timing and build out products or services. They are not creatives, however they can formulate the right questions, or as is more often the practice, adopt innovative concepts created by others.

By definition, the proclivity in architecture to hand over plans to builders creates innovators and cripples entrepreneurs. The single skill associated with the profession is the ability to visualise a structure and understand its use before it has been realised. This is a very special singular skill. In Italy, every design discipline begins its course of study under the pedagogy of architecture, not because every designer must know how to design a building, but to transmit the spatial and functional aptitude necessary for them to imagine structures that are yet to be built. This is more than design, and very close to the structure of innovation.

The single liability associated with the profession is the business of creating instructions for others to build from. It is central to the discipline and the reason why architects lack entrepreneurial skills and sensibilities. This is not to say they are not paid well or not shrewd businesspeople. Execution, realisation and implementation are simply outside of their standard scope of services. Simply stated: architects make plans; plans that others follow.

However, architects do not need to be innovative. In fact, adapting what is tested to the particularities of one-of-a-kind projects is challenging enough. Proven solutions paid for by entrepreneurs who assume the risk of delivering a built product to real people in real time satisfy the great majority of designers. The only foreboding risk to this business-as-usual approach is that it is exactly the type of professional work that artificially intelligent machines are very good at.

Structuring the Innovation Process

Becoming an innovator is expected and precedented, as all architects have hypertrophied visual imaginations. The MIT Media Lab was established in 1985 from within the architecture school by Nicholas Negroponte and Muriel Cooper. The skills of architects to ask the culturally relevant questions and to communicate their plans outwards is at the centre of the Lab's institutional mission. It is like an architecture school with the standard scope of services removed, but with the method of being creative intact.

Greg Lynn FORM,
Port Authority Triple Bridge Gateway,
New York,
1994

Competition entry for a new pedestrian bridge and gateway crossing 9th Avenue between 40th and 41st streets. This project was designed entirely using simulated physics in an animation environment where the structural curves were generated from trajectories of points moving through fields of attraction modelled on the site. Using special-effects software to simulate particle flow for drawing and modelling these dynamics was innovative at the time, as such tools were primarily only used by architects for rendering and animated fly-throughs.

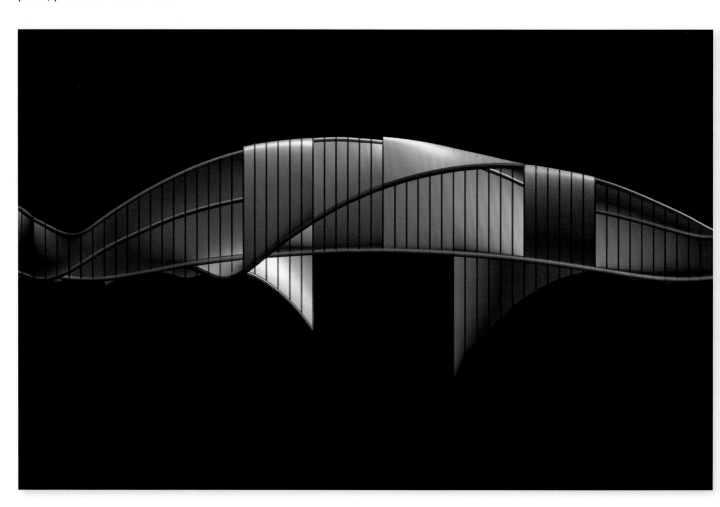

Another example of structured innovation put in place by an architect are the TED Conferences established by Ricky Saul Wurman. Similarly, the International Design Conferences in Aspen and the board of the Container Corporation of America that was the template for TED also understood that innovators, many of them architects, needed to ask the right questions that business could adopt to become more relevant, agile and entrepreneurial. Today one can regularly find architects in positions of innovation within companies or on their advisory boards.

New Mediums

Innovation often flows from the use of technologies in ways they were not intended. As an office involved with digital innovation, at Greg Lynn FORM, beginning in the 1990s, projects were designed using a digital rather than mechanically drafted medium. This is distinct from digital innovation in how designs were documented and delivered at the time, where CAD processes expedited mechanical drafting. For example, the Port Authority Triple Bridge Gateway competition entry (New York City, 1994) began with the use of simulated physics software for 3D modelling. The problem this project addressed was how to model context as gradient fields using gravitational force fields and project digital particles to derive dynamic trajectories for use as structural profiles. The same year, the Citron House commission in Long Island, New York, modelled the site as gradient fields of forces constrained by a flexible skeleton of fixed-length segments with limited stiffness and rotation at their joints.

An entrepreneur's skill is to understand culture in order to identify market opportunity, calibrate the timing and build out products or services

Greg Lynn FORM,
Citron House, Amagansett,
Long Island, New York,
1994

Proposal for a single-family house designed to take advantage of ocean views from an elevated site. The project used 'inverse kinematics' as structural constraints. In this innovative approach, the skeletons were used to deform rendered characters in the special-effects industry, and used in place of compasses and adjustable triangles for modelling masses on a site.

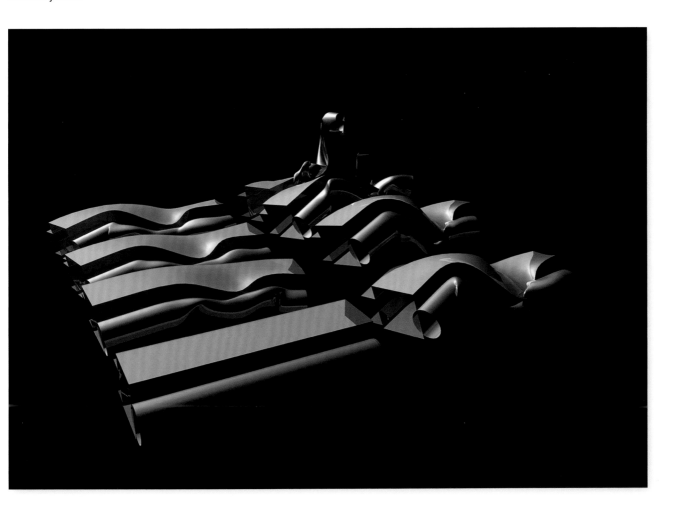

In these early projects there was a simple problem statement derived from digital techniques that could replace existing design tools. The Embryological House (1997) was the most robust project of this period that started with the simplest problem statement: 'Design many unique houses, to which nothing can be added or subtracted, and each of which is constructed of exactly the same number of parts.' Configurators were new at the time and were being used for combinations of colour, pattern and finish, but not for the design itself. This question led to a number of innovations including: the use of Maya Embedded Language (MEL) scripts and databases; procedural modelling operations; more than 50,000 unique house designs from the same family of interchangeable curves; thousands of 3D-printed models; hundreds of CNC-shaped moulds with vacuum-formed models; and enormous two-tonne models carved by CNC robotic arms. Additionally, a configurator with tens of thousands of solutions was launched as an interactive website. Innovations flowed from the simplest proposition.

Greg Lynn FORM,
Embryological House,
1997

The Embryolocial House was a self-initiated exercise to design a series of over 50,000 houses using the same number and types of components. Using a limited set of geometric variables and Excel spreadsheets feeding data into the MEL script editor of the animation tool Maya, a procedural workflow was invented to generate a controlled family of designs all with the same but not identical components. This approach would later become the basis for contemporary tools like Grasshopper used by architects for rationalising complex surfaces with similar non-identical components.

New Materials

Material innovation is closer to engineering and requires clear problem statements. The innovation challenge of the Vitra Ravioli Chair (2005) was part reduction and ergonomics. It led to a chair made of only a hard bottom and a soft top. The 3D-knitted upper was the first commercial use of this technology on a contoured seat, and eliminated 100 per cent of waste associated with upholstering. A similar process was used more than a decade later for the top surface of the Nike Microclimate Chair (2015–). The Alessi Tea and Coffee Tower (2003) used super-formed titanium in place of sterling silver, allowing grip detail using the tooling path of the graphite moulds; gradient colour using a custom jig and variable voltage as the part was lifted out of the anodising bath; a fraction of the weight and material of a cast part; and a more than tenfold increase in profit margins. In all three projects, the focus on material innovation led to an awareness of commercialisation, part count, tooling complexity, fabrication cost and retail sales margin. These concerns are outside the scope of services of a building design, but are central to the design and manufacture of consumer products. Sharing the risk, rewards and percentage of sales of these products as a partner rather than a design service provider is very different to the service fee business model. Industrial designers are closer to entrepreneurial processes than architects.

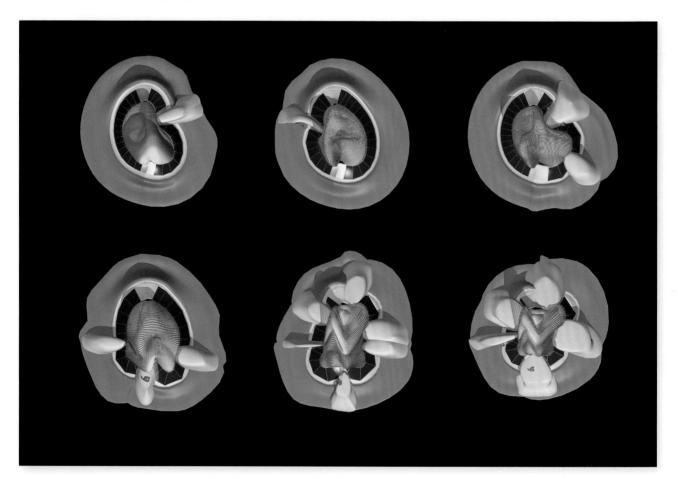

Greg Lynn FORM,
Vitra Ravioli Chair,
2005

The chair has two seating positions: one frontal with legs parallel
and arms supported on each side; the other at 60 degrees with an
arm thrown over the back and legs thrown over the groove where
the arms meet the back. The seating area is a single 3D-knitted
contour surface adhered to a foam structure. The base replaces
four legs with a single contoured fibreglass shell. The entire chair
is built from just two parts.

Greg Lynn FORM,
Nike Microclimate Chair,
2015

This intelligent chair optimises
athletes' performance in
preparation for, during and in
recovery from state-of-play in
NBA and college basketball
games. In the base of the chair
are custom-designed and
manufactured boards with
processors and controls for
heating, cooling, fans and user
interface including capacitive
touch controls and LED lighting.

New Scope

Similarly, technology companies are places where architects can learn the value of innovation to entrepreneurs as advisory board members. Serving on such boards of software companies like Caustic Graphics, MatterMachine and Gehry Technologies was an education in building a technical services and digital tool company, financing, shareholder agreements and acquisition negotiations.

Greg Lynn FORM's role at Curbside, a company positioned at the intersection of digital and physical shopping, was not project based, but instead that of design adviser for all physical structures including its deployable pick-up pods, Palo Alto office headquarters, and all other elements of the physical brand. Compensation was a combination of time and expenses with equity ownership. This investment in the success, cost and performance of the design and construction process meant that innovation and entrepreneurship were linked. Even after the recent acquisition of the Curbside by Rakuten, the mutual investment in design innovation and business relationships persists.

Greg Lynn FORM,
Curbside Pick-Up Pod,
2017

The pod is a branded, identifiable landmark for drivers, cyclists and pedestrians as they approach to pick up their parcels, hidden within which is a high-powered Bluetooth beacon for tracking customer location. The lower part provides shade for the employees as well as parcel storage. The entire structure is built from lightweight composites so that it can be mass-produced from one set of tools. Its light weight means it can be built with very large parts, reducing the assembly time and easing logistics so that it can be deployed in less than a day to various Curbside retail locations.

As co-founder and CEO of consumer robotics company Piaggio Fast Forward, the need to build processes and a business strategy around innovative plans is acutely apparent, encompassing market creation, supply chain, logistics, distribution, manufacturing, assembly, customer care and product development. The company is majority owned by Piaggio Group, the largest two-wheeled vehicle manufacturer in Europe, and maker of the Vespa among other lightweight vehicles. Piaggio Fast Forward was founded in 2015 with Jeffrey Schnapp and Michele and Roberto Colaninno, two recent architecture school graduates from MIT and Harvard, two graduates from the Rhode Island School of Design, a University of California, Los Angeles (UCLA) business school graduate, and a junior faculty member from Harvard. The first task was to define a large problem different from other mobility and robotics startups; a question that connects with the lifestyle legacy of the Vespa scooters, Moto Guzzi and Aprilia motorcycles that Piaggio designs, builds and sells. The robotics company is defined by 'Autonomy for Humans', involving machines that understand pedestrianism. More and more machines are beginning to move autonomously in the presence of people; however, the problem of human-machine interaction on sidewalks is more complex than how self-driving cars move on roadways. Where perhaps engineers can solve the challenges of autonomous cars sharing roads with human drivers, a more architectural and urban insight is required to design intelligent machines that move with people on sidewalks and in and out of buildings. The company needed to innovate new products with wheels that use following to move without being driven, and these are being rapidly commercialised for entrepreneurial consumer markets.

Architects' vision
and perspicacity
means they are
poised to become
innovators. Yet
they are trained
to believe their
work is finished
with the creation
of an original
idea, meaning
they lack
entrepreneurship

Innovator or Entrepreneur?

Experience in understanding the distinct domains of entrepreneurship and innovation is important. Architects' vision and perspicacity means they are poised to become innovators. Yet they are trained to believe their work is finished with the creation of an original idea, meaning they lack entrepreneurship. The work of an entrepreneur is not to be original or innovative. Even though entrepreneurs may look and sound like innovators and creatives, they rarely are. They are execution specialists who take on risk and responsibility in building companies in exchange for reward. More like developers than architects, they feed on innovation, but do not often create it. However, there are ways that architects can become more entrepreneurial: first, by automating parts of the existing scope of architectural services and replacing the expensive labour associated with the profession with machines that they design, engineer and own; and second, by getting out of the business of handing over plans to others for execution, and instead taking on the risk and possible reward of building and developing in addition to designing. ⌀

Piaggio Fast Forward,
gita robot,
2019

A hands-free carrier designed, engineered and manufactured at consumer robotics company Piaggio Fast Forward, co-founded by Greg Lynn. This is the first lightweight mobility robot designed for the consumer market to follow people on errands and neighbourhood trips to help reduce car usage, ride sharing and scooter rental. Often a gallon of milk, a yoga mat, several school books or two bags of groceries is the difference between a walking and driving trip. By using machine-vision and path-planning technology to autonomously follow a specific person while transporting up to 40 pounds (18 kilos), gita helps promote the active outdoor lifestyles people in the US currently desire.

On Reflection

Beautifully Disrupted Architectural Art

A Word from
△D Editor Neil Spiller

Brendan Neiland,
Embrace,
2015

The facade embraces its surroundings
to create a vista of shifting, disrupted
plates of colour, abstracting the figurative.

To live in London at the beginning of the 1950s was to inhabit a disrupted, soot and brick-dust encrusted, blitzed and meat-rationed existence. The younger generation of the time searched for something new, something optimistic and something exciting – and found it in fledgling rock and roll, advertising, magazines and movies. Above all, their focus was on America with its advanced consumer culture, supposed social mobility and the glitzy glamour of Coney Island, Hollywood, Times Square and Vegas. In such places, high- and low-code aesthetics, semiotics and messages of all kinds mingled in colourful strange positions. This mélange of imagery and forms inspired a group of young artists, architects, critics and theorists who from 1952 began congregating at London's Institute of Contemporary Art (ICA). Calling themselves the Independent Group, among their members were architects Alison and Peter Smithson, artists Eduardo Paolozzi, John McHale and Richard Hamilton, and writers and critics Lawrence Alloway and Reyner Banham. Their exhibited works reflected this fecund world of surreal encounters, scales and technologies.

The Parallel of Art and Life

The Independent Group's shows, as M Christine Boyer has written, 'displayed a non-hierarchical approach to imagery (mostly photographs), attempting to wring a new way of seeing things out of unusual juxtapositions'.[1] The Group's activities reached their crescendo in 1956 with an exhibition entitled 'This is Tomorrow' at the Whitechapel Gallery in London. This remarkable show consisted of 12 collaborating groups of architects, artists, sometimes engineers and others. One of those groups, but arguably the most important, included Hamilton, McHale and architect John Voelcker, aided and abetted by artist Magda Cordell (later to be McHale's wife) and others. The term 'Pop Art' stems from this group, although accounts differ as to its first use and attribution. However, Hamilton's view in 1957 was that Pop Art was popular,

transient, expendable, low-cost, mass-produced, young, witty, sexy, gimmicky, glamorous and big business.[2] He created the collage that would define this era.

Just what is it that makes today's home so different, so appealing? (1956), now in the Kunsthalle Tübingen collection in Germany, cleverly defines Pop Art visually exactly as Hamilton had also defined it in prose. It is a mirror of 1950s consumerist, social and sexual desire, a domestic interior strewn with consumer goods, electronic devices and modern furniture, with a bodybuilder holding a lollypop like a tennis racket advancing towards his Burlesque paramour. A contemporary memory theatre, it is full of pictorial references to the context and time within which it was made.

Brendan Neiland,
Rosanaline,
2015

In a genealogy that can be traced back to Dada and Cubism, disparate scaled objects are shown in juxtaposition, here facilitated by urban reflections and building facade topologies.

Pop Art's joy in the mirroring of disparate images of differing genus, and the pleasure it brings to its viewers, has permeated the modern world. Hamilton taught Peter Blake, perhaps most famous for The Beatles' *Sgt Pepper's Lonely Hearts Club Band* album cover (1967), who in turn taught English artist Brendan Neiland. Neiland's current work consists of great panoramas of fractured colour – paintings of reflections in modern city buildings, in the glass and mirror of the 21st-century metropolis. He seamlessly melds the present-day cityscape of commercial glass architecture with figurative clues and beautiful abstract cascades of mirrored colour and form. Modern Renaissance man, doctor of medicine, theatre and film director, and art critic Jonathan Miller, in the catalogue of the 1998 exhibition 'On Reflection' at the National Gallery in London, writes: 'the visibility of a surface is inversely proportional to its reflectiveness and … the more it discloses in the way of reflection the less it reveals itself as a surface.'[3] Reflections are virtual illusions; the more complex, kaleidoscopic and deep they are, the more they occlude the surface they reside in. They are dynamic, in a continuous ebbing-and-flowing relationship with the observer, defined by his or her individual point of view. Miller continues:

> It's significant that it was the mirror that brought about this conflict between the virtual and the actual. In contrast to the conventional systems of representation – pictures, diagrams, maps and models – the fidelity … is so great that the mirror is almost universally regarded as the epitome of representation.[4]

In Neiland's work, reflections bring about the disruption of the city and its momentary disappearance, where the virtual subsumes the actual in a hallucinogenic play of colour. High-code aesthetics blend into low-code aesthetics and are jump-cut by the mullions and transoms of curtain-walling. It is in this city phenomenon that Neiland, like his predecessors, finds a contemporary Pop Art play of form, colour and scales.

Aesthetic Encounters in the Contemporary City

Neiland's work has the overwhelming power of stained glass, but with a hyperreal luminosity created through his choice of vibrant colour and spray-gun painting technique. This hyperreality is conjured up consistently with the comic-book purity of line of Roy Lichtenstein's oeuvre. Though at face value this may seem paradoxical, straddling this line in fact helps give the work its engaging forthrightness. Some pieces also have a *Bladerunner*-esque language of neon and movie adverts, swivelling surveying eyes and promises of off-world paradises. The viewer, enchanted by these great bursts of colour, is seduced into accepting their bizarre disrupted reflections, mirrorings and semiotic cocktails. Yet these concoctions of everyday architecture and signs can be found in every city, every small-town watering hole or ubiquitous sleazy joint, and of course reach their apogee in Las Vegas, where one is reminded of Robert Venturi, Denise Scott Brown and Steven Izenour's 1972 classic *Learning from Las Vegas*,[5] a paean to speed and the accommodation of the car, and the expedient yet exuberantly decorated shed of the hotel or casino.

Brendan Neiland,
Blue Iris,
2017

Neiland's work also takes a pleasure in the human body, particularly eyes and lips, which are contrasted with less-organic forms.

Brendan Neiland,
Multiflections,
2014

opposite: In Neiland's paintings, the contemporary city is jump-cut and disrupted in the reflections of its own glass and mirrored facades.

Brendan Neiland,
Bouquet,
2017

In *Bouquet*, one is reminded, in a
contemporary Pop Art way, of Monet's *Water
Lilies* and the Cubist guitars of Georges
Braque and Pablo Picasso.

Neiland's art, like Vegas, is a world of face-
painted minxes, cowgirls, red lips and Coca
Cola, beer bottles, guitars and immortal
flowers, never to die until the electricity is
cut off.

Much has been written of the seminal position
in art history of Monet's *Water Lilies* as the
moment when modern painting passed from
the figurative to the abstract, which he caught
in a series of paintings that can be read as
either. The same might be said of Neiland's
work; however, the agent of his move from the
figurative to the abstract is the contemporary
city – it is his machine of creation, ever
flexing, ever combining, ever melting, aided
by the neon night. Neiland captures the dance
of colour and image, takes the dynamics of
time and sticks a pin in the accelerating city's
thorax, producing specimens plucked from its
invigorating panoramas.

British architectural journalist, publisher
and founder of the World Architectural
Festival, Paul Finch, has written about his
friend and near neighbour. He cites science's
understanding of the observer's effect on the

observed, and this phenomenon's intuitive
understanding within the art world: 'You see a
Neiland reflective streetscape and streetscape
will never be quite the same for you again,
because you have absorbed a way of looking/
feeling/thinking courtesy of an interaction
with artistic inspiration.'[6]

Psychic Mobility and Mirrors
The 'mirror stage' is a theory of the
psychological development of children
between 6 and 18 months old posited in
1936 by French psychoanalyst Jacques
Lacan. It is based on the belief that when
infants recognise their bodies in a reflective
surface (or other image source), they see
themselves for the first time as an object from
the outside. This, Lacan believed, becomes
human subjectivity or their sense of imagined
order. The child imagines what is in the mirror
to be a better version than the reality, which
can provoke feelings that we are not as 'good'
as our image as we compare our fragmented,
real selves with the perfect reflection.

The history of art, literature and cinema is
littered with a fascination for and exploitation

of the mirror, for example in the work of Salvador Dalí, Charles Dodgson, Diego Velázquez and a myriad of others. For French writer, poet, artist and filmmaker Jean Cocteau, the mirror was the doorway to another magical, metaphorical world, and he used it repeatedly in his work, particularly in the films *La Belle et la Bête* (1946), *Le Sang d'un poète* (1930) and *Le Testament d'Orphée* (1960). The mirror is also found in his numerous self-portraits and writings, in which he uses it as a device to understand himself, his creativity and sexuality. *Orphée* makes much of mirrors, their cracking and uncracking, the view from the magical space behind them with the trapped occupants of the real world trying to penetrate their metaphorical threshold. Lacan would have found Cocteau an interesting psychoanalytical study, for sure.

Viewers of Neiland's work are likewise captives in the contemporary city; through its mirrors we see another, perfect, prettier world, more colourful, more vivid, a cornucopia of image and symbol. Neiland's paintings show a world better than our world, the mixing pot of formal collisions and spectral palette making perfect storms of composition. From the middle to the end of the 1950s, the Independent Group's McHale made a series of collages of human-like heads and bodies. These 'Expendable Ikons', as he called them, consisted of the technologies of the day – pipes, valves, keyboards, electronic screens, ballbearings and spark plugs – and lent a powerful visual aesthetic to the idea of expendability. The constitution of our technological prostheses is forever changing our 'psychic mobility' (as McHale called it)[7] and fragmenting our extended anatomy. McHale's Ikons can be looked upon, now, almost as an archaeologist might view an antique artefact. They reveal layers of expendable technology, some forgotten. They are snapshots of the psychic mobility of the time, as is Neiland's work of his time. Neiland's fragmented, mirrored, kaleidoscopic, iconic and beautiful paintings with their cascades of colour offer visions of everyday life at the beginning of the

21st century that can be read by future archaeologists and art historians alike as a partial key to our contemporary disruptive existence as we navigate between the virtual and the actual and try to make sense of it all. ⌂

Notes
1. M Christine Boyer, *CyberCities: Visual Perception in the Age of Electronic Communication*, Princeton Architectural Press (New York), 1996, p 35.
2. Richard Hamilton's definition of Pop Art from a letter to Alison and Peter Smithson dated 16 January 1957
3. Jonathan Miller, *On Reflection*, National Gallery Publications (London), 1998, p 59.
4. *Ibid*, p 206.
5. Robert Venturi, Denise Scott Brown and Steven Izenour, *Learning from Las Vegas*, MIT Press (Cambridge, MA), 1972.
6. Paul Finch, *Brendan Neiland: Drawing on Life*, exhibition catalogue, Redfern Gallery (London), 2017, pp 4–5.
7. John McHale, *The Expendable Ikon: Works by John McHale*, exhibition catalogue, Albright-Knox Art Gallery (Buffalo, New York), 1984, p 10.

Brendan Neiland,
Stella Maris,
2016

Stella Maris further explores the reflective facade and its fragmentation of bodies and forms to create a kaleidoscopic, pixellated and beautiful work – at once sensual, but equally abstract.

CONTRIBUTORS

Sandeep Ahuja is the founder of building performance analytics firm Pattern r+d (the consulting arm of cove. tool). Most recently she presented at the UN Environment Assembly, with 1,500 global delegates, on the impact of building on climate change; showcased at TedxAtlanta; and won the Atlanta Startup Battle and Atlanta Power 30 Under 30 award for developing the automated sustainability consultant cove.tool. With her desire to bring automation into the AEC world, she is pioneering the integration of building performance within the design and construction process by developing and using intelligent technology and software.

Ben van Berkel studied architecture at the Rietveld Academy in Amsterdam and at the Architectural Association (AA) in London, receiving the AA Diploma with Honours in 1987. In 1988 he and Caroline Bos set up the architectural practice UNStudio in Amsterdam. UNStudio presents itself as a network of specialists in architecture, urban development and infrastructure. In 2018 he founded UNSense, which designs and integrates tech solutions for the built environment. He has lectured and taught at many architecture schools around the world. He currently holds the Kenzo Tange Visiting Professor's Chair at Harvard University Graduate School of Design (GSD) in Cambridge, Massachusetts.

Phil Bernstein is an architect, technologist and educator, and Associate Dean and senior lecturer at the Yale School of Architecture in New Haven, Connecticut, where he received his BA (honours) and MArch and has taught since 1988. He was formerly a vice-president at Autodesk, and prior to this a principal at Pelli Clarke Pelli Architects. He is the author of *Architecture | Design | Data: Practice Competency in the Era of Computation* (Birkhäuser, 2018) and co-editor (with Peggy Deamer) of *Building (In) The Future: Recasting Labor in Architecture* (Princeton Architectural Press, 2010). He is a Senior Fellow of the Design Futures Council and former Chair of the AIA National Contract Documents Committee.

Helen Castle is Publishing Director at the Royal Institute of British Architects (RIBA), where she oversees *The RIBA Journal*, book publishing and retail. From 2000 to 2018 she was Editor of *Δ*. Until 2016, she was also Executive Editor of the Global Architecture programme at Wiley, overseeing the US and UK lists. She was Head of Professional Programmes at the RIBA (2016–18). She has a BA in the History of Art and Architecture from the University of East Anglia, and an MSc from the Bartlett School of Architecture, University College London (UCL) in the History of Modern Architecture. She writes and talks regularly at events and schools of architecture.

Patrick Chopson focuses on the crossover between architecture and technology and leads the sales and marketing effort for cove.tool's cost versus energy optimisation to dramatically lower the cost of green buildings. With a background in mechanical engineering, architecture and high-performance buildings, he brings an integrated approach to help tackle the challenges of integration and optimisation. He is a licensed architect with over 10 years of experience in both architecture and mechanical engineering firms.

James P Cramer is the former Executive Vice President/CEO of the American Institute of Architects (AIA) and the founder of the Design Futures Council and DesignIntelligence. He serves on the faculty of the College of Design at the Georgia Institute of Technology in Atlanta.

Craig Curtis is Head of Architecture and Interior Design at Katerra. He received his BA in Architecture and BS in Construction Management from Washington State University. Known for his integrated approach to the design of high-performance buildings, he joined Katerra to help develop a seamless integration of architecture, engineering, manufacturing, supply chain and construction. In the past two years, the firm's design team has multiplied to more than 200, across multiple offices.

Daniel Davis is an independent researcher concerned with the relationship between people, space and design technology. He originally trained as an architect in New Zealand and later completed a PhD at RMIT University in Melbourne. He worked as a senior researcher for CASE Inc, and after its acquisition by WeWork, became WeWork's director of research, establishing and managing the team through a period of hyper growth. His research has appeared in a variety of publications, including *WIRED* and *Fast Company*, and he is a regular columnist for *Architect* magazine.

Jared Della Valle is the founder and CEO of Alloy. He has been a real-estate professional and architect for more than 20 years, and has managed the design, acquisition and predevelopment of more than two million square feet in New York. He is Board Chair of the Van Alen Institute, and also sits on the Board of the Architecture League of New York. He has taught and lectured at major universities and institutions, and his work has been the subject of more than 150 articles and publications. He holds a BA from Lehigh University in Bethlehem, Pennsylvania, and Master's degrees in both architecture and construction management from Washington University in St Louis, Missouri.

David Fano is Chief Growth Officer of WeWork, where he leads global real-estate, design, construction, sales, marketing and data initiatives. Trained as an architect, his interests and expertise lie in connecting technology and data within the building industry. He studied at Columbia University's Graduate School of Architecture, Planning and Preservation (GSAPP) in New York before joining SHoP Architects as Director of Technology Research. He went on to become the CEO of CASE Inc., a consultancy he co-founded prior to joining WeWork.

Frank Gehry was raised in Toronto, but moved with his family to Los Angeles in 1947. He received his Bachelor of Architecture degree from the University of Southern California in LA in 1954, and studied city planning at Harvard GSD. In subsequent years he has built an architectural career that has spanned over five decades, and produced public and private buildings in the US, Europe and Asia. His work has earned him several of the most significant awards in the architectural field, including the Pritzker Prize.

Meaghan Lloyd is the Chief of Staff and partner at Gehry Partners, a full-service architectural firm with extensive international experience in the design and construction of academic, museum, theatre, performance and commercial projects. She also served as CEO of Gehry Technologies, a cloud-based software and service company for the architectural, engineering and construction sectors, from 2012 until 2014, when she presided over the merger of Gehry Technologies with Trimble Inc. She was elected to their board of directors in 2015.

Greg Lynn is the founder and owner of Greg Lynn FORM and co-founder and CEO of Piaggio Fast Forward. He is a professor at the University of Applied Arts Vienna, and at UCLA. He was the Davenport Professor at Yale University from 2000 to 2016, and has also taught at Harvard (2017–18), Columbia (1992–9) and the ETH Zurich (1999–2002). He won a Golden Lion at the Venice Architecture Biennale, and the Architecture Award from the American Academy of Arts and Letters. He is the author of 13 books.

Jesse Louis-Rosenberg is an artist, computer programmer and maker. In 2007, he co-founded Nervous System, of which he is Chief Science Officer. He is interested in how simulation techniques can be used in design and in the creation of new kinds of fabrication machines. He studied maths at the Massachusetts Institute of Technology (MIT) and previously worked at Gehry Technologies in building modelling and design automation.

Jessica Rosenkrantz is an artist, designer and programmer, and co-founder and Creative Director of Nervous System. Her work explores how simulations of natural processes can be used in design, and coupled with digital fabrication to create one-of-a-kind customised products. She studied biology and architecture at MIT and Harvard GSD. Nervous System's designs have been featured in a wide range of publications, including *WIRED*, the *New York Times* and the *Guardian,* and are part of the permanent collections of the Museum of Modern Art (MoMA) and Cooper Hewitt Smithsonian Design Museum in New York, and the Museum of Fine Arts Boston.

Brad Samuels is a founding partner and Director of Research at SITU, an unconventional architecture practice located in Brooklyn. He works on a range of projects, from agile, community-oriented spaces for the Brooklyn Public Library to mixed-use masterplanning in the Hudson Valley. He also directs SITU Research, where architectural and spatial tools intersect with human rights advocacy. A Fellow of the Urban Design Forum, he is on the board of the Architectural League of New York and Technology Advisory Board for the International Criminal Court. He holds a Bachelor of Arts from Vassar College in Poughkeepsie, New York, and Bachelor of Architecture from the Cooper Union in Manhattan.

Marc Simmons is a founding principal at Front. He is also Associate Professor of Practice at MIT, and the past Ventulett Chair of Architectural Design at the Georgia Institute of Technology. He is a licensed architect in New York State, and holds a Bachelor's degree in environmental studies and a professional Bachelor's degree in architecture. With 25 years of experience, his specialist facade knowledge is built upon previous work at Foster + Partners, Meinhardt Facade Technology and Dewhurst Macfarlane & Partners.

Scott Simpson, formerly CEO of The Stubbins Associates in Cambridge, Massachusetts, is a Richard Upjohn Fellow of the AIA and a Senior Fellow of the Design Futures Council. He teaches at the Advanced Management Development Program at Harvard University.

Chao Yan is a postdoctoral researcher at Tongji University in Shanghai where he collaborates with Professor Philip F Yuan to conduct research on the history of construction technology and digital design theory. He is also currently a visiting lecturer at the China Academy of Art in Hangzhou. His work focuses on the intersection between architectural theory and philosophy, and he has published extensively on the history and theory of the body, neurophilosophy in architecture, and post-1968 architectural history.

Philip F Yuan is the founder of Shanghai-based Archi-Union Architects and Fab-Union Technology, and a professor at Tongji University. His research and practice involve the application of prototypical methods and advanced manufacturing techniques, focusing on how digital tools offer the possibility of a new authorship for today's architects based on an understanding of culture, materials and the built environment. His research and projects have received many international awards, and been exhibited worldwide, including at the 2018 Venice Architecture Biennale, 2017 Chicago Architecture Biennial, Milan Triennale, Urbanism\ Architecture Bi-City Biennale (UABB) of Shenzhen and Hong Kong, and the Shanghai Biennial, and have formed parts of several renowned museum collections.

What is *Architectural Design*?

Founded in 1930, *Architectural Design* (△) is an influential and prestigious publication. It combines the currency and topicality of a newsstand journal with the rigour and production qualities of a book. With an almost unrivalled reputation worldwide, it is consistently at the forefront of cultural thought and design.

Each title of △ is edited by an invited Guest-Editor, who is an international expert in the field. Renowned for being at the leading edge of design and new technologies, △ also covers themes as diverse as architectural history, the environment, interior design, landscape architecture and urban design.

Provocative and pioneering, △ inspires theoretical, creative and technological advances. It questions the outcome of technical innovations as well as the far-reaching social, cultural and environmental challenges that present themselves today.

For further information on △, subscriptions and purchasing single issues see:

http://onlinelibrary.wiley.com/journal/10.1002/%28ISSN%291554-2769

Volume 89 No 2
ISBN 978 1119 500346

Volume 89 No 3
ISBN 978 1119 546023

Volume 89 No 4
ISBN 978 1119 506850

Volume 89 No 5
ISBN 978 1119 546245

Volume 89 No 6
ISBN 978 1119 546214

Volume 90 No 1
ISBN 978 1119 540038

How to Subscribe
With 6 issues a year, you can subscribe to △ (either print, online or through the △ App for iPad)

Institutional subscription
£310 / $580
print or online

Institutional subscription
£388 / $725
combined print and online

Personal-rate subscription
£136 / $215
print and iPad access

Student-rate subscription
£90 / $137
print only

△ App for iPad
6-issue subscription:
£44.99 / US$64.99
Individual issue:
£9.99 / US$13.99

To subscribe to print or online
E: cs-journals@wiley.com

Americas
E: cs-journals@wiley.com
T: +1 781 388 8598
or +1 800 835 6770
(toll free in the USA & Canada)

Europe, Middle East and Africa
E: cs-journals@wiley.com
T: +44 (0) 1865 778315

Asia Pacific
E: cs-journals@wiley.com
T: +65 6511 8000

Japan (for Japanese-speaking support)
E: cs-japan@wiley.com
T: +65 6511 8010
or 005 316 50 480
(toll-free)

Visit our Online Customer Help available in 7 languages at www.wileycustomerhelp.com/ask